FROM

ANCIENT EGYPT TO CHAGALL & PICASSO

UNDERSTANDING ART

———————

PEOPLE, THINGS,
and IDEAS

UNDERSTA

FROM ANCIENT EGYPT TO CHAGALL & PICASSO

NDING ART

PEOPLE, THINGS, and IDEAS

LUISE C. KAINZ

Chairman of Art, Washington Irving High School, The City of New York

OLIVE L. RILEY

Director of Art, Board of Education, The City of New York

HARRY N. ABRAMS, Inc.,
Publishers, New York

FRONTISPIECE. Dance at Bougival. *Pierre Auguste
Renoir (French, 1841-1919). Museum of Fine Arts, Boston, Mass.*

Library of Congress Catalog Card Number: 66-11012

HARRY N. ABRAMS, INC., NEW YORK

Printed and bound in Japan

CONTENTS

PEOPLE, THINGS,
and IDEAS

1

What Art Can Do

SINCE THE DISTANT DAYS of the past, man has created many kinds of art. In drawings, paintings, and sculpture he has recorded his ideas and feelings about the world in which he lives. Impressions of his fellow men and their activities, of his gods, his religious beliefs, and the emotions they aroused in him have been and still are subjects that concern artists.

You may wonder about early man and what he was like. What have scholars done to find out about him? Since no written language existed in prehistoric days, they have had to study all types of ancient art to learn about man's past. Archaeologists have dug far below the surface of the earth to uncover fascinating remains of primitive and ancient civilizations. They have unearthed entire cities, villages, dwellings, caverns, and graves. The innumerable objects discovered there help us to piece together exciting stories of people who lived thousands of years ago. Through these discoveries we have learned much about the way of life of our earliest ancestors. Archaeologists continue their search. They are sure that many more treasures still remain all over the world.

Archaeologists' curiosity and deep interest in man's past have provided our museums with vast collections. These collections help us to write the history of ancient times. They reveal to us early man's desire for art quality in even the most ordinary articles and necessary implements for daily use. With an instinct for beauty, these people from the distant past decorated their ceremonial garments, their religious and ornamental objects, with painstaking care and attention to detail. They were fine, instinctive craftsmen. Their

9

PLATE 1. King Khafre. *Egyptian, about 2500 B.C. Stone, from the Temple of the Pyramid of Khafre. Museum, Cairo (Egypt)*

paintings and carvings surprise and delight us with their skill and imaginative qualities. Seeing these and many other forms of art created by early man increases our understanding of the extent and importance of our art heritage.

The artists of today, like those of the past, continue to record the history of their time. They show us how people look, what they wear, and what they do. Through their creations, we see people in their daily occupations, in games, sports, dances, parties, and other colorful, exciting activities. Artists continue to describe and interpret their particular surroundings, whether these be crowded cities, silent forests, teeming jungles, or stormy seas. Together, the artists of the past and present have helped paint a portrait of life itself. They have helped us to understand and appreciate the vast extent of man's eternally creative spirit.

ART REVEALS CHARACTER

This book is designed to show you how art has grown out of the interest of painters and sculptors in people and their activities. We shall start by showing you how skillfully the artist can interpret character. He not only has insight into the physical features that suggest the dominant characteristics of a person, but he has also the skill to capture them in some medium of art. A fine sculptor, for example, working in resistant stone or pliable clay, can suggest the individuality of a person so convincingly that the lifeless material in which the image is made seems to be alive.

Let us look at a few of the many different kinds of people whose appearance and character have been captured by the mind, eye, and hand of the sculptor.

First you see how an artist from ancient Egypt characterized a king who ruled over his subjects almost three thousand years before our time. The head of a statue of *King Khafre* (Plate 1) shows us a godlike character of unmistakable power and authority. The sculptor has purposely emphasized the rigid pose and simplified the features. Notice that he has omitted any natural irregularities that might lessen the majesty of the statue. A pleated headdress, shaped somewhat like the steps of a pyramid, adds greatly to the king's regal dignity. Horus, the sun god, under whose protection King Khafre ruled, is symbolized by the falcon behind his head. This impressive, beautifully carved bird clearly conveys the belief that the king had a divine protector.

11

PLATE 2. Rider's Head. *Greek, about 550 B.C.*
Marble, excavated on the Acropolis, Athens.
The Louvre, Paris (France)

In creating this truly monumental figure, the sculptor followed the Egyptian belief that the preservation of an individual's likeness would help him to exist forever.

Far more friendly and human than the portrait of the Egyptian King Khafre is that of an ancient Greek citizen (Plate 2), who lived during the time when Greece was the center of culture and civilization. You can clearly see that the head and shoulders of this man are more relaxed in pose and spirit than those of the Egyptian king. While the sculptor has carved the features simply, they are neither remote nor rigid. The hair and beard have been executed in a conventional style that was characteristic of the sculpture of this period. This Archaic, or early, period of Greek sculpture seldom fails to suggest a thoughtful serenity and humanity characteristic of the man of early Greece.

It is interesting to note that a few years after this Greek head was found, the torso was unearthed on the Acropolis. It was then recognized that head and torso were part of an almost life-size horse and rider.

12

The bronze portrait (Plate 3), supposedly of Julius Caesar and made by a Roman artist about 50 B.C., two thousand years ago, shows us still another form of the sculptor's art. Notice how much more lifelike it is than the Egyptian and Greek sculptures. This realism has two causes: the sculptor's desire to create an image that came close to the sitter's actual appearance, and the fact that the model for this sculpture was probably made in moist clay. This material, as you know, is very pliable and therefore permits the sculptor to work in greater detail than he can in stone or wood.

This is a portrait that vividly brings out the subject's personality because it emphasizes the facial characteristics that best reveal the nature of a great and powerful man. The intelligence, determination, and aggressiveness of a conqueror are all suggested by the way the sculptor has modeled and stressed the various features. Deep lines in the forehead and around the mouth show the effects of heavy responsibilities. This portrait not only suggests the greatness of the hero who conquered Britain and Gaul but it also gives evidence of the cares and worries that such a man might endure.

Sculptors from primitive civilizations often used their talents to portray

PLATE 3. Portrait (Julius Caesar?). *Roman, about 50 B.C. Bronze. National Museum, Rome (Italy)*

PLATE 4. Ghost Mask. *New Caledonia, Southwest Pacific Ocean, probably late nineteenth century. Wood, with hair and feathers. Rautenstrauch-Joest Museum, Cologne (Germany)*

PLATE 5. Head of a Girl. *Aristide Maillol (French, 1861-1944). Bronze. The Museum of Modern Art, New York, N.Y. (Gift of Mrs. John D. Rockefeller, Jr.)*

characters who, although imaginary, played an important role in their lives. Some of the most fantastic art in existence came from these sculptors whose world was inhabited by a host of invisible and usually threatening spirits. To portray these unseen powers, the primitive sculptor often carved images in the form of masks. These masks were worn to enable a witch doctor or tribesman to make sudden and startling appearances at ceremonies intended to placate or to call forth the spirits they represented.

The ghost mask (Plate 4) from New Caledonia, an island in the South Pacific, portrays a supernatural character most effectively. Although in general the features look human, the nose resembles a bird's beak, and the mouth suggests that of a ferocious animal. Strongly carved lines on the cheeks add to an impression of awesome power.

The tall headdress, wiglike hair, and feather collar show the primitive sculptor's ability to combine native materials skillfully and effectively. Undoubtedly fear and superstition guided the hand of the primitive sculptor, as it did that of the Egyptian artist. However, these twin forces did not prevent him from producing sculpture of great strength and effectiveness.

Primitive sculpture, particularly African sculpture, has strongly influenced some modern artists. They greatly admire its dramatic simplicity and unusual use of materials. It is interesting to note that many a highly trained artist wishes that he had the directness and power of the primitive and usually untaught artist.

The *Head of a Girl* (Plate 5) is the work of Aristide Maillol, a famous French sculptor who died not long ago. What do you think the artist wanted to tell us about this young person? She appears to be thoughtful and serene, in spite of her youthfulness. The head is solidly formed, with few surface details. A roll of hair frames her attractive, simply modeled features.

Like the earlier Roman head that you have just seen, this head was also modeled in clay, then cast in bronze by a rather complicated process. The beautiful quality of the bronze is brought out by polishing the surface so that it picks up and reflects brilliant highlights.

Color, in the usual sense, does not play an important part in sculpture. However, the three-dimensional quality of carved or modeled forms enables us to grasp the ideas of the sculptor through the power of light and dark contrasts, created by the play of lights and shadows on the forms he has created.

It is important to remember that in sculpture the unified and harmonious relation of all details to the large mass helps to give it a monumental quality. This quality is characteristic of all great sculpture.

ART DRAMATIZES MOODS

We should always keep in mind the fact that an artist does not merely reproduce what he sees. Since the true artist is a creative person, his eyes do not operate like the lens of a camera. Everything he sees is affected by his mind, his emotions, and his feelings. This is why he has the special qualities that enable him to create works of art. One of these qualities is his highly personal way of seeing and reacting to people, places, and things. Another quality is his ability to retain his impressions of what he sees and to arrange and rearrange them through the media of paint, clay, stone, and a wide variety of other materials.

Let us look at a few paintings to see if we can discover how the artist has used these two qualities or talents to interpret a subject in his own, individual way. *Blowing Bubbles* (Plate 6) was painted by Jean-Baptiste Chardin, an eighteenth-century French painter. Notice how the quiet, intent attitude of the young man is brought out by the curving lines that enclose his figure and bring our eyes down to the slowly forming, delicate bubble. At this point, our attention is drawn to the expressive face of the fascinated child.

You will notice that the colors used by the artist are subdued and mainly quite dark. The lighter tones are reserved for the face and hands of the young man. These skin tones are warmer in hue than the tones to be seen in the less important background areas of the painting.

Chardin was always interested in suggesting weight and solidity in his paintings. Every part of the young man's figure makes you feel its three-dimensional quality. He was interested in textures, too, as can be seen in the carefully painted hair and the glossy bubble.

The pose of the figure, the dramatic placing of the bubble, and the subdued color all contribute to the quiet, yet suspenseful mood that Chardin wished to convey.

Details of pictures painted in the past remind us that fashions in clothing and hair styles change throughout the years. While the young man's costume differs only in a few details from one worn today, his long, bow-tied hair would startle us if we were to meet him face to face.

Let us now look at *The Gourmet* (Plate 7) by Pablo Picasso, a Spanish painter who lives and works in France. Although one color, a greenish blue, has been used extensively, Picasso varied it in many different ways. His use of this cool color gives the painting a decided mood. A subtle contrast of glowing, warm light illuminates the areas of the head and hands. As you can see, this contrast brings them out very effectively. Through the pose and action of the little figure, one can sense the child's concentration on the all-important task of feeding himself.

It will be interesting for you to look for the similarities and differences to be found in these two paintings, *Blowing Bubbles* and *The Gourmet*. In each the artist suggests mood by means of color, using cool tones throughout the painting and retaining the warmer hues to emphasize the head of his subject. In both paintings we are made aware of the bulk and structure of the figures.

An obvious difference between the two paintings can be seen in the artists' brushwork. Chardin worked more slowly and liked the appearance of a smooth-surfaced canvas, while Picasso, on the other hand, used a much more vigorous brush stroke. In each case the artist's technique has reinforced his theme.

ART USES MANY MEDIA

One important asset that the artist brings to his work is the ability to express his ideas through the forceful use of an art medium. Whether he chooses paint, clay, stone, wood, or any other of the wide variety of materials used by artists, he must control and master it to express his ideas effectively. Sometimes his control appears so effortless that we lose sight of the skill of his hands and eyes.

The artist is also sensitive to the particular creative possibilities of each medium. For example, he knows that watercolor, a very fluid medium, demands quick, sure handling. He also knows that oil paint can be used in many ways that range from the traditional technique of the old masters to the more experimental handling of the medium by present-day artists. Whether traditional or experimental in his use of a medium, the artist always needs to understand the chemistry of paints in order to secure permanency for his works. Many of the paintings of the old masters have seriously deteriorated through unfortunate choices and combinations of colors and materials. To-

PLATE 6. Blowing Bubbles. *Jean-Baptiste Chardin (French, 1699-1779). Oil on canvas.*
The Metropolitan Museum of Art, New York, N.Y.

OPPOSITE: PLATE 7. The Gourmet. *Pablo Picasso (Spanish, born 1881). Oil on canvas.*
The National Gallery of Art, Washington, D.C. (Chester Dale Collection)

day's artists are very much aware of this fact and are intensifying their study of the use of the new painting media now being produced as a result of recent research and new testing devices.

In the field of sculpture, each medium has its own particular qualities. The sculptor who selects stone or wood in which to carve his subject is well aware of their potentialities for rugged or smooth surfaces and of the special qualities of their native color and texture that he may use to advantage. The sculptor also knows when to select a more responsive medium, such as clay or wax, if the nature of wood or stone would prove resistant to his ideas. Then, too, since we are in an experimental and pioneering age, the present-day sculptor is especially challenged both by the idea of using traditional materials, such as copper and brass, in new ways and by the idea of using new media, plastics and other synthetic materials, for the creation of sculptural forms that particularly express the spirit of his contemporary world.

2

The Artist's Familiar World

SEEING THE WORK of many artists makes us realize their intense interest in their surroundings and in the people they see enjoying simple pastimes, working, or moving about in their environment. Sensitive artists find a great deal in daily life that challenges them. They are very much aware of the fact that familiar scenes offer excellent subjects for drawings and paintings.

The eye of the artist, of course, is more highly trained than that of the average person. The artist sees intensively and selectively. He brings sympathy and understanding to the people, objects, and scenes he selects for the subject matter of his paintings. The way he interprets what he sees is the result of his interest in particular qualities and characteristics that may or may not be apparent to other observers.

When we first look at various paintings, they may seem quite realistic or lifelike to us. However, after careful study, we can see how the eye, mind, and hand of the artist have changed the actual appearance of his subject. We can then realize that he interprets a subject as he pleases. He may choose to suggest the peaceful, the dreamlike, or the poetic, or he may prefer to stress that which is dramatic, harsh, or even bitter.

INTERPRETING IN HIS OWN WAY

Let us look at the work of Jan Vermeer, a seventeenth-century Dutch painter. In all of his paintings, he communicates the mood of the familiar household scene of his time. With great understanding of the home-loving

PLATE 8. The Cook. *Jan Vermeer (Dutch, 1632-1675). Oil on canvas. Rijksmuseum, Amsterdam (Holland)*

PLATE 9. I and the Village. *Marc Chagall (Russian, born 1887). Oil on canvas. The Museum of Modern Art, New York, N.Y.*

people he knew so well, he takes us into a world of quiet, modest, and contented living.

The Cook (Plate 8), one of his masterpieces, shows us how he used tones, or values of color with great effectiveness. Notice, for example, the wide range from light to dark on the background wall area. Sunlight streaming in through the window on the left is used to great advantage in modeling the sturdy figure of the cook, who is contentedly preparing a meal.

In contrast to the serene and warmly human appearance of the cook in her quiet kitchen, the people in *I and the Village* (Plate 9) are represented far less realistically. Marc Chagall, a Russian-born artist who has worked most of his life in Paris, enjoyed re-creating the world of his childhood. In this painting he brings a fairy-tale quality to a remembered village in old-time Russia. We can enjoy the gay color and the whimsical way in which Chagall took liberties with the actual appearance of his subject. A green-faced peasant stares at a multi-colored cow that, the painter suggests, may be remembering a friendly milkmaid. A field worker and his companion are apparently on their way to work. We cannot be certain just why the woman is floating through the air rather than walking. Possibly Chagall thought of her as so happy that she no longer felt earthbound. Memories of the houses in his quaint village have been drawn upon to give the background scene an almost theatrical quality. Chagall has drawn and painted them in a deliberately childlike way. Two of the houses are upside down and behind the window of another there appears an oversized face intently viewing the colorful scene.

You have studied two paintings, one of a scene that the artist saw as quiet and peaceful, the other revealing the artist's love of fantasy. As a third example of the varied ways in which artists may choose to interpret subject matter, look at *The Passing Scene* (Plate 10) painted by Jack Levine, a contemporary American painter. It clearly reveals Levine's sharp reaction to poverty and the depressing life of the slums. Just as we have writers who raise their voices in protest against injustices in our social order, so we have painters who also hope to persuade people to remedy them.

You will find in this painting that the artist has used distortion very effectively. He has distorted, or exaggerated the natural proportions of figures.

OPPOSITE: PLATE 10. The Passing Scene. *Jack Levine (American, born 1915). Oil on composition board. The Museum of Modern Art, New York, N.Y. (Mrs. Simon Guggenheim Fund)*

PLATE 11. The Card Players.
Paul Cézanne
(French, 1839-1906).
Oil on canvas.
The Louvre, Paris (France)

Study them carefully. Consider the size and shape of the man's head and
hands, for example. Do they help to suggest his character? What other ideas
has the artist used in his painting to convey his message?

Paul Cézanne, one of the greatest French artists of the nineteenth century, was also a painter of familiar scenes. In his own words, this artist's
greatest purpose was "to realize" the actual inner forms of his figures, landscapes, and objects by painting them as even more rugged than they are in
reality. His great understanding of the many qualities of color helped him
accomplish his purpose.

A study of Cézanne's paintings reveals a complex organization of lines,
planes, and color surfaces. This organization is known as the structure of a
painting. "Structuring" a painting is an important part of the work of an
artist. Cézanne's original method and style of painting have had a wide influence on many artists, even to the present day.

The Card Players (Plate 11) shows two figures that form a compact
structure, almost rocklike in its firmness. The unity and close relationship
of all its parts make the composition strong and tightly knit. Cézanne painted
several versions of this subject; the one shown here is very well known. You
will find it interesting to study the use of color in this painting. Within each

26

color area you will discover the many variations of colors that Cézanne used to convey a feeling of space and solidity.

Vincent van Gogh, a nineteenth-century Dutch painter who worked chiefly in France, is a master whose paintings are highly prized by our generation. When he was a young man living in northern Holland, he devoted himself to studying and painting the people of that region. He was so moved by the hard life and poverty of these people that he could think of little else. In many drawings and paintings, he recorded the activities of the peasants at work in the fields and in their homes. During this early period Van Gogh expressed the thought that "An artist must have a warm heart for his fellow men," and he stated his intention of devoting his life to expressing the poetry hidden within their lives.

The Potato Eaters (Plate 12) is a stirring expression of Van Gogh's sympathy for his hardworking countrymen. The most striking aspect of the

PLATE 12. The Potato Eaters. *Vincent van Gogh (Dutch, 1853-1890). Oil on canvas. Collection V. W. van Gogh, Laren (Holland)*

painting is the emotional quality that its creator is famous for conveying. Deep, somber, heavy colors have dramatized an everyday scene and made it memorable.

JUDGING PAINTINGS

Certain basic principles are helpful in evaluating works of art, no matter what period in history they come from. Of course we can always think or say, "I like this painting but I don't know why." However, we may find even more enjoyment when we look at beautiful paintings with an understanding that goes beyond a casual glance. For this kind of experience, we need to know something about the qualities that are considered essential to fine painting.

Sensitivity to these qualities will be strengthened by repeated study of the fine paintings of many periods of art. It becomes increasingly apparent that masterpieces show certain underlying similarities. Your first likes or dislikes may change as you gradually come to recognize the important qualities that distinguish a great work of art. When a painting has a meaning for you that is apart from the story it tells, then you are probably becoming more knowledgeable and experienced in looking at art.

What are some of the qualities you may expect to find in a painting? As we mentioned previously, the power with which an artist expresses an idea, a mood, or a particular feeling for his subject is of primary importance.

If color is the most important element used by the artist, then you might need to study first the quality of the color: its variety, harmony, tonal range, and balance. You would then think about the ways color has been used to suggest form, space, or mood. Every painter selects and distributes and applies color in a completely individual manner. The way he plans the interplay of light and dark, and creates an interesting pattern of color, also helps him produce an expressive work of art.

A third factor to look for in painting is the way the artist has organized his work. This means that you need to consider the arrangement of the important elements that make up the painting: line, color, form, space, and texture. If you study each element separately, you will see how each has been treated to heighten the expression of the subject. You will also see how each element is related to the others and how the artist has welded them all into a unified whole, or composition.

3

Art in Early Times

In PREHISTORIC TIMES, art was the way in which primitive man found he could best explain many ideas. Lacking a large vocabulary of spoken words and not having developed a written language, he naturally turned to the most direct form of communication. This was expressed by drawing, carving, and painting his activities, both real and imagined.

The art of early and prehistoric times, when compared with that of later and modern civilizations, is often surprising to us. We find many of the same basic qualities present in great art of every period. Prehistoric man has shown us his remarkable powers of observation and memory. His art was completely original: he was guided not by what people had done before him but by his own vision, his own will, and his own ingenuity. He has also shown us his skill in making and using tools. Primitive art in its own way is as stirring as many other forms of art from later and more highly cultured periods of history.

The struggle for food in the early days of civilization was of the greatest importance and was often fatiguing and dangerous as well. We have been left many records of this struggle, beginning with those made by the first known artist, the cave man. Such records have been found on clay and stone walls deep in caves and rock shelters in many parts of the world. Among them are amazing hunting scenes painted with colored earths. Painting animals and human figures served several purposes, the most important of which was magic. It seems that the cave man believed that making an image of his prey placed the animal under his power.

There is reason to believe that these paintings and scratched drawings,

PLATE 13. Jumping Cow. *Prehistoric rock painting, about 20,000 B.C. Cave, Lascaux (France)*

PLATE 14. The Struggle over a Bull. *Prehistoric rock painting, after 10,000 B.C. Libya (Africa)*

aside from their magic meaning, provided a means of teaching boys how to fight, hunt, and prepare food. Today we may see many reproductions of paintings and drawings from the Ice and Stone Ages that are as fresh and vital as many of our modern paintings. It is amazing that they were done so many thousands of years ago.

One of the most exciting records of prehistoric art came to us with the discovery of the paintings in the Cave of Lascaux in France. It is difficult for us to realize that its superb and well-preserved wall decorations were painted over twenty thousand years ago. The animals, in groups reminiscent of hunting scenes, are almost terrifying in their vitality, as you may observe in Plate 13.

From the Libyan Desert in Africa has come another forceful and exciting rock painting (Plate 14). This also shows the extraordinary ability of primitive artists to dramatize an event which must have been a common one in their savage lives. Two rival groups are struggling for the possession of a bull. The fight is dramatically depicted by the men's figures, which the artist has painted so simply and clearly. Amusingly enough, and contrary to his generally accepted character, the bull is not enraged.

When we talk about the primitive artist, we can hardly speak of him as having only a slight knowledge of art and its techniques. As you have seen in his drawings and paintings, he has an amazing feeling for artistic expression. In addition, he was skilled in inventing and using art processes, even though they may seem quite simple to us today. Just imagine yourself as a prehistoric cave painter. Could you have made your paints and brushes? Could you have managed to work deep in the heart of a gloomy cave, lighted only by a feeble torch of your own making? And, more important, could you, without any knowledge of similar kinds of art, have managed to create paintings that still stir the world with their forcefulness?

Let us now consider the work of a later people, the Egyptians, who advanced far beyond their uncivilized predecessors. They have left us many forms of art that are still vital because of their striking originality and their expression of a way of life.

EGYPT

Early accounts of Egyptian life, recorded in picture writing, or hieroglyphics, can be readily interpreted by scholars today. A study of the magnificent art of the ancient Egyptians, their huge temples, powerful sculpture, countless wall paintings, and relief carvings, tells us much of their daily life, religious ideas, and beliefs. When designing and working in many materials, the Egyptian artist had to follow strict rules that were laid down for him by his Pharaohs and priests. Although these rules set the style of art, they did not prevent the artist from producing superior work. Even today Egyptian art impresses us with its powerful and often monumental quality.

Murals (paintings on walls), reliefs (sculpture attached to a background), and free-standing sculpture were important forms of art from the beginning of Egyptian civilization. However, the murals found in tombs, or burial places of the nobility and other important personages, were not painted for the enjoyment of visitors. Like the sculpture that is also found there, the primary purpose of the murals was to keep the spirit of the deceased alive and comfortable in the afterworld. In Egypt the painter, the sculptor, and the architect all served the belief that the spirit could live after death, provided that the body, or an image of it, and pictures or statues of servants, food, and other earthly needs were preserved in the tomb.

Egyptian artists followed a prescribed way of drawing the human figure. A profile view of the head, legs, and feet, a front view of the shoulders, and a front view of one eye always appear in their paintings. This way of showing a figure may seem rather odd to you. However, to the Egyptians, it was completely satisfactory since it clearly revealed the structure of the figure as they knew it to be, rather than as they saw it.

Lady Reciting Prayers over Table of Offerings (Plate 15) shows a young girl clad in a thin garment and wearing the traditional Egyptian wig secured by a headdress. Gold jewelry, for which Egyptian craftsmen were famous, can be seen in the bracelets, wide collar, and earrings she wears. Her hands are raised in a beautiful gesture above the offerings of food and flowers intended to sustain the spirit of the deceased on its long journey toward a new life. The mural is simply painted in flat colors delicately outlined to emphasize the figure. The striking note of the black wig attracts our attention immediately.

The Nobleman Hunting (Plate 16) is another handsome example of

OPPOSITE: PLATE 15. Lady Reciting Prayers over Table of Offerings.
Egyptian, about 1400 B.C. Copy of wall painting in Tomb of Menena, Thebes.
The Metropolitan Museum of Art, New York, N.Y.

PLATE 16. The Nobleman Hunting. *Egyptian, about 1450 B.C.*
Wall painting, fragment. British Museum, London (England)

Egyptian mural art. The figure of the nobleman dominates the scene, for he appears twice, on either side of the papyrus grove. On the left side he is hunting birds with a boomerang, and on the right side he is spearing fish. His family and members of his household are with him, some to assist him and some, it seems, to enjoy themselves by picking bouquets of lotus flowers. Everybody appears to be having a good time.

Below the light reed boats, the waters of the Nile seem to part in zigzags, to show us fish, waterfowl, and water flowers. Observe how successfully the artist has arranged the many elements—people, boats, fish, flowers, and numerous birds—according to what they do and where they are. The smoothly flowing line leads our eyes from one part to another and knits all these elements into a compact whole.

The Funeral Ceremonies (Plate 17) is also complex and rich in design. The mummies of two men are being purified by zigzag streams of water, before the mummies are placed into the actual tomb, which is behind, at the

34

right. Portrait masks are being fitted onto the mummies. At the left is a priest, and the sorrowful women embrace the feet of each mummy. The empty space is filled with funeral flowers and with picture writing, or hieroglyphics, that tells about the ceremonies. This scene was part of a larger wall decoration in the tomb of the two men seen here as mummies.

ASSYRIA

Other civilizations, contemporary to that of Egypt, developed in nearby Asia in an area known as the Valley of the Two Rivers or the Tigris-Euphrates Valley. Although nature's forces have destroyed the massive and imposing temples, palaces, and fortresses, a great deal of magnificent sculpture remains to tell us of the power of successive generations of artists.

The Assyrians, who inhabited the upper part of the valley three thousand years ago, used vast areas of sculptured reliefs to ornament their buildings. The *Winged Being* (Plate 18) was found by archaeologists in the ruins of the palace of Ashurnasirpal II. Here we see represented a familiar deity of this time. A powerful being, apparently he arrived on earth from time to time in order to give a stately greeting.

PLATE 17. The Funeral Ceremonies. *Egyptian, about 1350* B.C. *Painted chest. Museum, Cairo (Egypt)*

PLATE 18. Winged Being. *Assyrian, about 880 B.C. Alabaster relief. The Metropolitan Museum of Art, New York, N.Y.*

PLATE 19. A Prince. *Cretan, about 1600 B.C. Wall painting. Museum, Heraklion (Crete)*

CRETE

The island of Crete in the Mediterranean Sea gradually developed a civilization that became the forerunner of Greek art. At the beginning of our twentieth century, excavations of luxurious palaces built under the rule of the Minoan kings brought to light many and varied art treasures. These objects, now in our museums, attract and fascinate many visitors by their beauty and skilled workmanship.

Geographic location and climate have always played an important part in shaping the temperament and thinking of a people. This is particularly true of the artists of Crete. During the two thousand years of their history they developed many forms of art that are eloquent records of their happy, pleasure-loving existence. The splendors of the royal palaces, with their furnishings and vivid murals, are outstanding evidences of a brilliant culture.

The murals found on Crete and at Mycenae on the Greek mainland, where there was a culture related to that of Crete, show interesting signs of the conventions that were used in Egyptian figure drawing. You will notice this in the picture, *A Prince* (Plate 19). While his head is shown in profile, the eye is in a front view and his figure is shown in a combination of side and front views. With his small waist, flowing locks, and elaborate headdress, the prince is a graceful figure. The curved lines of the lilies through which he walks emphasize the decorative quality of this painting.

In addition to their mural paintings, the Cretans produced sculpture that has great artistic merit. This sculpture, as well as their pottery, greatly influenced the work of their neighbors on the Greek mainland.

GREECE

Even the earliest examples of Greek art show pronounced differences from the Egyptian style. Both religion and climate played a part in humanizing Greek art, that is, in helping it to present the living rather than to immortalize the dead.

A vivid and independent imagination led the Greeks to create amusing legends about their gods and other deities. They thought of them as descending from above, mingling with mortals, and entering into dramatic and fanciful adventures. Many of the Greek myths we read today are concerned with these adventures.

Characteristically, the Greeks had an eager, individualistic strain that led them to high levels of creative thinking in art, science, and literature. They were by nature sensitive to beauty and made its creation and enjoyment an important and necessary part of their lives.

It was a Greek ideal to become or to create the perfect individual, one of heroic skill and physical perfection. Athletes spent their lives training their bodies; artists sought endlessly to represent gods and goddesses, heroes, and men and women in terms of perfect physical beauty. This constant striving to represent the ideal person is characteristic of Greek art.

The mountains and surrounding islands of Greece contained many types of beautiful marble, an ideal material for carving. Working directly in this medium, their sculptors produced superb free-standing and relief sculpture, designed chiefly to adorn their temples.

The relief sculpture, *Women Dancing* (Plate 20), represents two figures in rhythmic movement. Throughout the entire arrangement there is a thoughtful, studied repetition of varied line arrangements. Verticals echo verticals; angular lines are carefully balanced. Even the folds of the women's garments are arranged to repeat and reinforce the varied line directions. One becomes conscious of the sculptor's skill at describing restrained poses and suggesting the motions of a dance by the harmoniously flowing drapery. Throughout his composition, the artist conveys a feeling of serenity and dignity.

Heracles as an Archer (Plate 21), on the following page, represents this god in human guise, engaged in a human activity. How physically strong and ideally perfect he appears! Despite the complicated pose, there is a feeling of freedom and ease of movement in the figure. With bow powerfully drawn, the god clearly marks his target. The perfect sense of balance achieved by the sculptor once more reveals the Greek ideal of poise and calm within the bounds of action.

Pottery is another form of art that the Greeks brought to high perfection. Their vases and jars, made primarily to store food and liquids, were handsomely painted in red, black, and white designs. These told stories from life, described daily occupations, and recorded heroic struggles. Like a modern illustrated news report, these pieces of pottery give us an animated picture of Greek life, interests, and activities. Although fashions and customs have changed in the more than two thousand years since this type of pottery was made, we still feel close in spirit to the people of early Greece. This is

PLATE 20. Women Dancing. *Greek, about 510 B.C. Sandstone relief from the Temple of Hera. Museum, Paestum (Italy)*

PLATE 21. Heracles as an Archer. *Greek, about 490* B.C. *Marble, from pediment of the Temple of Aphaia, Aegina. Glyptothek, Munich (Germany)*

PLATE 22. Marriage Procession, from a Black-Figured Vase. *Greek, about 540* B.C. *Pottery. The Metropolitan Museum of Art, New York, N.Y.*

apparent when we study the vase shown in Plate 22 and see the sharply drawn, lively, and expressive movements of the figures painted on it.

ETRURIA

The Etruscans, who lived in a part of ancient Italy called Etruria, produced many forms of art that bear an interesting relationship to some of those produced by the artists of Greece. Their sculpture, especially, reminds us strongly of archaic Greek forms. Etruscan art has the strength and vitality that comes from artists who work independently and who use art as a direct language of expression. Activities of war and peace were often the subjects for vigorous sculpture and mural paintings. Although few of the actual facts of their history are known to us, we can readily see that Etruscan civilization was highly developed. Their art forms show us that these people had a fresh and active outlook on life.

The Etruscan *Horseman* (Plate 23) is one of four figures that ornament the top of a bronze wine container, made about 500 B.C. The Etruscans developed the art of bronze sculpture to a high degree. Their skills in this difficult art were inherited by their successors, the Romans. By turning to page 13 and again studying the Roman sculptured head, you can see that the Romans developed an even greater technical mastery of bronze casting.

The small horseman is shown at the moment of releasing an arrow from his bow. Opposing diagonal line movements, made by the bodies of the horse and rider, clearly suggest their mutual strength and vitality. The rider's helmet, in the form of a swan's neck and head, adds a distinctive note to his appearance.

In their mural paintings the Etruscans show us that rigid rules and formal poses did not dominate in their work as they did in that of the Egyptians. The *Flute Player* (Plate 24), painted to adorn a tomb, reveals a carefree, joyous spirit; in pose the figure suggests lighthearted action. Rhythmical movement in its decorative design reflects the theme of music and dance. We can see that the Etruscans observed people without idealizing them and that a love of living is expressed in their art.

PLATE 23. Horseman. *Etruscan, about 500 B.C. Bronze figure from the cover of a wine jar.*
British Museum, London (England)

OPPOSITE: PLATE 24. Flute Player. *Etruscan, about 480 B.C. Fresco painting in the Tomb*
of the Leopards. Tarquinia (Italy)

4

Art as Spiritual Expression

THE SPREAD OF CHRISTIANITY, toward the end of the Roman Empire, marks
a new phase in the story of art. It became an all-important means of education, bringing new ideas to people who could neither read nor write. Artists
and craftsmen were called upon to devote their various talents to the service
of the Church. In order to teach people the true meaning and significance
of the new religion, they deliberately emphasized the spiritual qualities rather
than the material aspects of their subjects. These early Christian artists did
not copy nature or use models to make the figures that they painted or carved
appear more lifelike. Their subjects, which were from the Bible or told stories
of the saints, were expressed with the utmost simplicity and clarity. The
artists relied on their own religious convictions to convey spiritual content.

To grasp the extraordinary abilities of the early Christian artists, let us
study the mosaic type of decoration that preceded the paintings produced
by later artists. *The Three Magi* (Plate 25) is a Byzantine mosaic, so called
because its style originated in Byzantium, the city that under the rule of
Emperor Constantine became the capital of the Roman Empire. As you
may know, a mosaic is a design created by setting small pieces of colored
stone or glass into wet cement, which then hardens and holds them in place.
Mosaics, rich and glowing with color and gold, provided highly effective wall
decorations for the early Christian churches. *The Three Magi* is both beautiful in design and superb in color, as well as being a vital expression of
religious devotion. The movements of the richly patterned figures suggest
their eagerness to reach their destination.

PLATE 25. The Three Magi.
*Byzantine, 500-526 A.D. Mosaic,
portion, decorating the nave.
Church of Sant' Apollinare
Nuovo, Ravenna (Italy)*

PLATE 26. St. Peter Preaching to the People. *Fra Angelico (Italian, 1387-1455).
Fresco painting. Museum of San Marco, Florence (Italy)*

PLATE 27. Flight into Egypt. *Giotto (Italian, 1266?-1337).*
Fresco painting. Arena Chapel, Padua (Italy)

PLATE 28. The Journey of the Magi. *Sassetta (Italian, 1392?-1450). Tempera on wood.
The Metropolitan Museum of Art, New York, N.Y.*

PLATE 29. The Tribute Money.
*Masaccio (Italian, 1401-1428).
Fresco painting (portion) in the
Brancacci Chapel. Santa Maria
del Carmine, Florence (Italy)*

Because mosaic, by the very nature of its materials and processes, restricted the ways in which artists could interpret subject matter, they began to experiment with paint as a means of conveying their religious messages. This change in media resulted in the birth of painting in the Western World.

GIOTTO

Giotto, an Italian painter who lived during the late thirteenth and early fourteenth centuries, was the first of the many great artists of the city of Florence. He made of painting such a powerful art that his work influenced contemporary and succeeding painters, establishing him as a great master.

A legend concerning his childhood tells us that while he was tending sheep, he passed away the hours by drawing pictures of sheep on flat slabs of stone. The Florentine painter Cimabue, who happened by and saw the drawings, was amazed by their excellence. He persuaded the boy's father to allow him to take Giotto into his workshop as an apprentice. There the young boy began with the ordinary work of sweeping floors, grinding pigments, and learning the rules of mosaic work. In his free time he drew from life and explored the new art of fresco painting.

While still young, Giotto received a commission for a fresco painting. In this process, tempera-like paints are applied directly to a coat of plaster freshly spread on the walls. This was the chief process used at that time to decorate the large areas of wall space in the interiors of the churches of Italy. Many of these paintings may be seen today, in an excellent state of preservation.

Compared with the Byzantine mosaic you have just seen, Giotto's frescoes display greater liveliness and more individuality of expression. With sure strokes and great courage, he created masterpieces that were convincing and inspiring. To this day, they are outstanding examples of early painting.

Giotto discovered, as you can see, how to make figures look lifelike and how to suggest form and depth in painting. In studying his *Flight into Egypt* (Plate 27), one sees that he constructed it as an architect would plan a building. Each area, whether it is part of the background or the foreground, is given a definite shape that is clearly defined and closely connected with each neighboring area. This kind of organization gives the whole painting a basic structure that intensifies the feeling of strength and dignity expressed by the figures.

In this same work, one clearly sees how Giotto stressed the important lines of the figures and of the mountains in the background. By repeating these vertical, horizontal, and diagonal lines he gives a sense of movement and rhythm to the entire composition. No small details or surface ornaments distract us from the all-important pious attitudes or from the nobility of the figures.

FRA ANGELICO

This artist was a noted and beloved Florentine painter of the fifteenth century. He entered a holy order and painted religious scenes with complete devotion and earnestness. A monk secluded from the world, Fra Angelico worked in the tradition of the Middle Ages, relying on his imagination rather than on a study of real life to create his figures. He communicates a feeling of the happiness of the spirit, giving to his art a sacred earnestness.

Saint Peter Preaching to the People (Plate 26) shows a kinship with the work of Giotto. A strong feeling for the compositional arrangement of figures is apparent. Balanced and varied groupings, carefully planned, lead our eyes easily to the important figure of Saint Peter. Notice how the gestures of his hands unify the figures, many of whom are dressed in the costumes of the period. Just as Giotto placed his figures in a clearly designed background, so Fra Angelico included an architectural setting that adds a new note of realism to the scene.

SASSETTA

Sassetta, another fifteenth-century painter, lived in the Italian town of Siena. Unlike many other artists of his time, Sassetta did not share the urge to make forms appear more true-to-life. He has made us richer by paintings in which he shows us, with touching devotion, the pageants that took place in honor of the saints.

Sassetta created these scenes as if they were taking place in his own day rather than many centuries earlier. In the *Journey of the Magi* (Plate 28), the rich costumes worn by the nobility, the scenery of his own country, and the customs of its people are closely interwoven with the religious story he is telling. The figures may seem childlike and simple in drawing, but this helps to make their meaning and expressions all the clearer. The artist's feeling for line and for splendid surfaces makes his paintings highly decorative. His traditional use of gold, together with clear, brilliant areas of light and dark colors, results in a painting of great richness.

The work of the thirteenth- and fourteenth-century painters had led their successors slowly toward the discovery of new possibilities for painting. They became more aware of the importance of the individual and more concerned with placing him within his own, living world. In the work of a young and highly talented painter, we can clearly see some of the new directions that painting was to take.

MASACCIO

This artist is considered an extraordinary genius for, although he died at about the age of twenty-eight, his paintings foreshadow a very different kind of painting. This may best be seen by a comparative study of Fra Angelico's *Saint Peter Preaching to the People* (Plate 26) and Masaccio's *The Tribute Money* (Plate 29). You will probably notice immediately that the latter painting does not have the doll-like, graceful quality of the former. In *The Tribute Money* all of the figures are solid and massive in form. Highlights and shadows play over them and keep our eyes traveling from one to another. Moving light also filters throughout the background, making the distant mountains both convincing and impressive. Deep, rich color adds greatly to the dramatic quality of the scene.

THE GOLDEN AGE

A period of supreme achievement in man's artistic activities was reached in the time of the Renaissance during the fifteenth and sixteenth centuries. While the literal meaning of the term Renaissance means rebirth, it can be truly stated that the wealth of art produced during this period was not simply a revival of interest in past accomplishments. The intense activity and idealism of highly talented Renaissance artists, combined with their striving for perfection, may have been given an impetus by their study of Greek and Roman art. However, the tremendous strides made in general learning at this time opened up entirely new fields of knowledge. The Renaissance, often

OPPOSITE: PLATE 30. The Virgin of the Rocks. *Leonardo da Vinci (Italian, 1452-1519).*
Oil on wood, now transferred to canvas. The Louvre, Paris (France)

called the Golden Age, was a time of eager experimentation and of a restless search for practical knowledge. The period when the Renaissance reached the heights of its artistic powers brings to our minds many illustrious names, among them Leonardo da Vinci and Michelangelo, the notable Italian artists, and El Greco, the Greek who became one of Spain's most famous painters.

LEONARDO DA VINCI

Leonardo, the "perfect painter," is one of the immortals of art. While it is true that he left us fewer paintings than most of his contemporaries, there remains the volume of his drawings, writings, and inventions to testify to his genius as well as to his superb draftsmanship. We have ample proof of his mastery in many fields of research, such as mathematics, geology, engineering, anatomy, perspective, and other sciences. A poet as well as an artist and an inventor, he saw little difference between art and science. His mind was clear, deliberate, and powerful in his intellectual search for beauty and for perfection in the painter's art. As a person his presence aroused wonder and admiration, while the clarity and directness of his writings led the reader to a better understanding and appreciation of his paintings. Leonardo da Vinci accepted only those aspects of the world that he discovered for himself, and he based his art on these discoveries.

In looking at Leonardo's *The Virgin of the Rocks* (Plate 30), we see figures placed in the half-light of a dusky grotto. Their harmonious arrangement is based on a triangular, or pyramid-like shape that holds them in a compact group. Strong highlights and deep shadows lend an air of mystery and solemnity to each holy person. Leonardo's intense interest in human forms, in the ways they can be painted to appear more lifelike, and in the special quality of their movements and gestures can readily be seen. His sensitivity to the importance of the movements and gestures of his subjects may be read in a statement that he wrote about painting. He said there, "What should be asked first in judging whether a painting be good is whether the movements are appropriate to the mind of the figure that moves." If you study the hands in this painting, you will see how each individual gesture has been used to reveal the spiritual quality and character of an individual.

In this painting, an illusion of depth and space was created through Leonardo's knowledge of perspective and his unique handling of light and

PLATE 31. Moses. *Michelangelo Buonarotti (Italian, 1475-1564). Marble,*
from the Tomb of Pope Julius II. Church of San Pietro in Vincoli, Rome (Italy)

shade. The use of poetic color in the upper left of the painting helps to suggest a distant landscape.

MICHELANGELO

This genius of the Renaissance was younger than Leonardo da Vinci, and survived him by many years. According to the custom of the times, Michelangelo, a silent and moody boy, was apprenticed to a master painter. His own desire for a more exact knowledge of the human figure led him to an intensive study, not only of the works of painters, such as Giotto and Masaccio, but also of Greek and Roman sculpture. At an early age his mastery in representing human anatomy, in all its complexity of structure and movement, was widely acclaimed. Commissions for mural paintings, such as those for the Sistine Chapel in Rome, and for important sculptural monuments poured in. His energy seems to have been boundless. Even the immense physical labor of painting the ceiling of the Sistine Chapel, that took him over four years to complete, or of carving huge blocks of marble did not daunt him in the least.

When Michelangelo first addressed himself to the task of carving a human figure, it is said that he felt or saw the figure within the block. With hammer and chisel, he then proceeded to "release" the figure from its rigid confines. In all of the many sculptures carved by Michelangelo, we can sense both the tremendous creative force and the superb craftsmanship of an unrivaled genius.

In the heroic pose of *Moses* (Plate 31), we can grasp the powerful concepts that moved Michelangelo to create this masterpiece. It seems that there could be no clearer expression of the controlled intellectual and physical energy of a superior being. The magnificent carving does more than attain beautiful surfaces of flesh, muscles, and drapery for within the very stone itself there seems to be the movement and breath of pulsating life.

EL GRECO

Domenikos Theotocopoulos, best known as El Greco, or "The Greek," is another example of an unusual, highly personal genius. Born on the Greek

OPPOSITE: PLATE 32. The Nativity. *El Greco (Spanish, 1541-1614). Oil on canvas. The Metropolitan Museum of Art, New York, N.Y.*

54

island of Crete, he went to Venice to study the work of the late Renaissance painters. Finally he settled in Toledo and actually became the first of the great painters of Spain.

Like many artists of his time, El Greco was a devout man who felt within himself the need to describe sacred stories through the medium of paint. In composition, in color, and in his use of moving, rhythmic figures, he departed from the accepted style of the Italian masters. Highly original, he created a world of his own inspired by his own fiery spirit.

The Nativity (Plate 32) is a stirring and dramatic scene. An inner light which seems to come primarily from a central source, the figure of the Child, gives the painting an unusual brilliance. The expressiveness of each figure is further emphasized by flamelike patterns of darting light and rich yet muted color. The agitated movements of the figures with upraised arms lead us into a world of mysticism and ecstasy. The figures themselves are made all the more expressive by El Greco's manner of lengthening them beyond their normal proportions and by modeling them in extremes of light and shadow.

ARTISTS IN OTHER WORLDS

You have seen some examples of the way in which art in the Western World served religion from the sixth through the sixteenth centuries. In many Eastern countries, in China, Persia, and India, for example, during these and at even earlier times, art became a highly accomplished expression of various spiritual beliefs.

Let us think of ourselves as in China during the ninth century. The prevailing religion at that time was Buddhism, brought from India by missionaries and eagerly embraced by the people. A succession of anonymous Chinese painters and sculptors continually produced works of art that reflected the enduring religious fervor of their various times. Among their works were figures of Buddhist deities, including Bodhisattvas, or "little Buddhas," that even to us today seem to be endowed with noble and serene personalities.

Kuan Yin (Plate 33), the Bodhisattva of Compassion, is a warmly appealing figure, relaxed, contemplative, and kindly. Carved from wood during the ninth century, it was painted in rich color touched with gold. Traces of these colors still add to the emotional appeal of this figure that has survived for over eleven centuries.

An equally interesting, although very different example of the arts of the East that were concerned with spiritual beliefs may be seen in the Persian manuscript painting, *Jonah and the Whale* (Plate 34). The finest of Persian painting is to be found in handmade books of the fourteenth, fifteenth, and sixteenth centuries. During this time, as in the days of the Renaissance in Italy, artists were employed by wealthy patrons. The shahs of Persia included in their courts many painters and calligraphers, who were specialists in the art of beautiful handwriting. Their duties included copying and illustrating the famous books of those times. The Koran, the sacred book of the Mohammedans, contained the Old Testament story of the prophet Jonah, and this tale was illustrated in tempera paint by a Persian artist of the fourteenth century.

Here we see Jonah who, after emerging from the body of the whale, is reaching for a garment that is being brought to him by a swiftly flying angel. While the figures bear the stamp of Persian painting, you may notice that the whale resembles the Chinese or Japanese paper fish that we may see and buy in this country today. The flat, decorative treatment of all the elements in the painting and its fresh, bright color, have a direct, childlike quality.

During the sixteenth century in India, a reigning emperor established his capital as an important center of learning and of art. More than one hundred Persian and Hindu court painters were trained under his rule and they produced books of surprising beauty.

Krishna Holding Up Mount Govardhan (Plate 35) is a color reproduction of a handsome miniature painting made during this period of artistic activity. The subject is based on a Hindu epic legend. Krishna, the central figure, was a widely worshiped deity of the Hindu religion. He is shown at a dramatic moment. In levitation, that is when he is rising in the air without support, he is also lifting the mountain so that his people may take shelter beneath it. Thus, through his extraordinary power, they are spared the torrential rain sent down by Indra, the jealous rain god.

There are many interesting details to be observed in this small painting. They include the relative sizes of the figures, ranging from that of Krishna to the much smaller people sheltered beneath the rocks, the way the worshipers are placed around Krishna, and the variety and richness of the flat and shaded colors.

In the south of India, Siva was a very important figure in the Hindu religion. In sculptured form he appears in the different roles assigned to him

PLATE 33. Kuan Yin.
Chinese, T'ang Dynasty,
seventh to tenth centuries.
Painted wood.
The Metropolitan Museum
of Art, New York, N.Y.

PLATE 34. Jonah and the Whale. *Persian, fourteenth century. Tempera on paper, illustration in a manuscript. The Metropolitan Museum of Art, New York, N.Y.*

LEFT: PLATE 35. Krishna Holding Up Mount Govardhan. *Indian, sixteenth century. Tempera on paper, illustration in a manuscript. The Metropolitan Museum of Art, New York, N.Y.*

by Brahma who was considered the supreme being and creator of the Universe. In the bronze sculpture *Siva as Nataraja* (Plate 36), he appears as Lord of the Dance. A forceful, superbly balanced figure, his pose and action suggests to us a dancer who will be forever in motion.

The four arms traditionally given to Siva represent the four aspects of his being. In one hand you can see a small drum which represents the first sound of creation. The opposite hand holds a flame, a symbol of destruction. The third hand is upraised in a protective gesture, while the fourth points toward a small dwarf who signifies the evil overcome by the Lord of the Dance.

The high headdress adds importance to Siva's head, while the linear pattern of the flamelike shape behind it suggests a god's supernatural power.

PLATE 36. Siva as Nataraja (Lord of Dancers). *Indian, fifteenth century. Copper. Museum of Fine Arts, Boston, Mass.*

5

Art for Prosperous Townspeople

THE DEVELOPMENT of independent countries and free city-states through commerce and trade contributed to the growth and importance of a new class of people, namely prosperous businessmen or merchants. These people became an important source of wealth and influence in the changing social and political life of Europe in the sixteenth and seventeenth centuries. Compared to the limited number of palaces in which sovereigns and nobility lived, there were now many fine houses for the newly wealthy. This was particularly true in Germany, Holland, and Flanders.

These citizens wished to show not only their wealth and standing in the community, but also their cultivated taste in choosing the best art for themselves. The kind of art demanded by these prosperous people took on a more worldly form. It was both possible and highly desirable for every man to beautify and enrich his dwelling with works by the finest artists and craftsmen.

At this time artists were organized into guilds or unions. They had huge workshops and, with the help of their apprentices and students, were able to fill many orders for paintings, decorations, and objects of all kinds. Portraiture became especially popular. Every citizen of means commissioned an artist to paint a likeness of him and members of his family. Then, too, wealthy officials ordered large paintings and group portraits to decorate their town halls and other public buildings. Because of widespread interest and a commonly shared respect for art, there was always a challenge for the artist to maintain the high standards of his craft.

PLATE 37. Peasant Dance.
Pieter Bruegel
(Dutch, 1525/30-1569).
Oil on wood.
Kunsthistorisches Museum,
Vienna (Austria)

PLATE 38. Peasant Wedding. *Pieter Bruegel (Dutch, 1525/30-1569).*
Oil on wood. Kunsthistorisches Museum, Vienna (Austria)

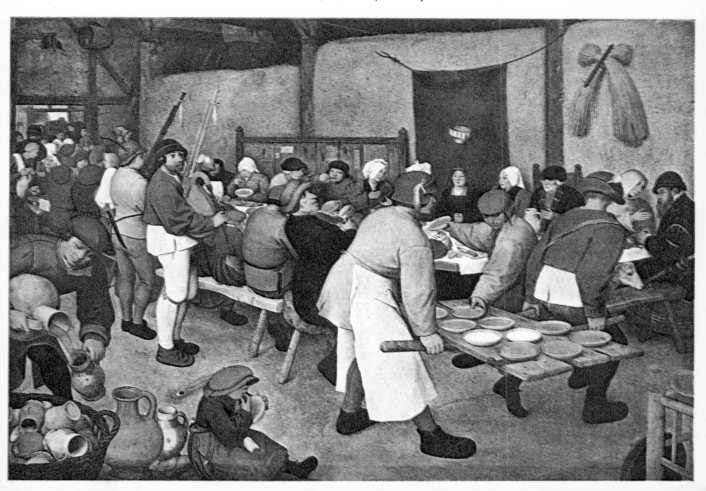

PLATE 39. The Four Horsemen of the Apocalypse. *Albrecht Dürer (German, 1471-1528).*
Woodcut. The Metropolitan Museum of Art, New York, N.Y.

ALBRECHT DÜRER

This artist was a celebrated German painter and graphic artist in the early sixteenth century. A drawing Dürer made of himself at the age of thirteen convinced his father, a goldsmith, that his son should become an artist, rather than follow his own profession. He was therefore apprenticed to a master artist of Nuremberg. After four years of study and work, he set forth as a journeyman artist, according to the rules of the medieval guilds.

Dürer was filled with the desire to increase his knowledge in every possible way. True to the Renaissance spirit, he not only painted but he also worked in the related fields of architecture, designing fortifications and monuments, and he also wrote about his opinions on various theories of art. In addition, Dürer illustrated countless books and pamphlets. His travels through Germany, Switzerland, and the Netherlands, and his visits to Venice added to his understanding of the spirit of his times.

Gutenberg's invention of the printing press toward the middle of the fifteenth century had stimulated the production of prints for book illustration. As a master of the woodcut and the copper engraving, Dürer remains unsurpassed. His *Four Horsemen of the Apocalypse* (Plate 39) shows his great skill both as a draftsman and as a graphic artist. This print is from one of the first woodcuts that achieved the precision, detail, and the intricate line and tonal quality of an engraving. Study the subject carefully. It presents a scene of violent action. In accordance with a description in the Bible, Dürer has shown in great detail the four horsemen who represent the ravaging forces of conquest, slaughter, famine, and death.

PIETER BRUEGEL

In the sixteenth century, a flourishing period in art, Bruegel attained a leading place as a master painter of the life and people of the Netherlands. His paintings are as important and meaningful to us today as they were to the people of his time. We are carried back to the atmosphere and mood of the peasants as they dance and celebrate in a gay fashion. More clearly than words can reveal, Bruegel's paintings describe the character, customs, and spirit of his Flemish countrymen. He observed them as individuals and he studied them in crowded groups. A masterly talent for selecting expressive poses and actions distinguishes his work. Unusually keen, beautifully simplified drawing, marked by a flowing quality of line, and thoughtfully balanced color are always to be found.

Less is known of Bruegel's personal life than we usually know of other artists of this time. Judging by the amount of work he produced in a lifetime of only forty-four years, it is clear that he was a prodigious worker. His family of sons and even grandsons followed in his footsteps, but Pieter Bruegel the Elder remains the most outstanding of all.

It is said that Bruegel often joined his countrymen in their gay activities, participating wholeheartedly in their ways and enjoying their humor. We sense this as the artist, in his *Peasant Dance* (Plate 37), takes us into the midst of a lively village scene. The remarkable drawing of the figures, both near and far, their carefree movements and delightful details, impress us immediately. In this painting, as well as in the one below it, Bruegel has

PLATE 40. Hunters in the Snow. *Pieter Bruegel (Dutch, 1525/30-1569). Oil on wood. Kunsthistorisches Museum, Vienna (Austria)*

placed the small figure of a child in the lower left-hand corner. This device, in effect, intensifies for the viewer the size and bulk of each of the centrally placed main figures. There is a refreshing humor and spiciness in this scene of happy, boisterous people.

In his *Peasant Wedding* (Plate 38), Bruegel shows his sympathy, understanding, and human feeling for the many interesting types of persons assembled in one colorful scene. However, the perfection of his art is never marred by mere storytelling effects. His work retains its lively pace because of his insight into the characteristics of each figure. He draws each one of them in the pose that is the most usual and understandable. In terms of design, by alternating reds, blues, and whites with yellows and smaller areas of green, he builds a strong, rhythmic color pattern that unites all parts of the canvas into a masterful tapestry of life.

Bruegel's landscapes, like his paintings of people, faithfully retain the character of his environment. Despite the influence of Italian painting on the artists of the Netherlands, he always asserted his individualism, and his power of seeing the essential truth of things never diminished. Looking at *Hunters in the Snow* (Plate 40), we feel drawn into this scene as if we were standing at the entrance of a large, spacious building. This effect has been achieved, not by painting in a realistic or "photographic" manner, but by the planned and conscious intentions of the artist who composed and drew with knowledge and vision.

The structure of the landscape, with trees, figures, distant mountains, and objects, is put together as if built on a precise, mathematical formula. This is exactly what the artist used. Each part is related and leads to adjoining parts. There is an absolute harmony of all small forms within the entire space. Even though it is carefully planned, the effect it conveys is that of a living, natural scene.

We may think of Bruegel as a painter who was attracted only to the gay side of life. Yet certain of his paintings reflect the deep compassion he felt for those of his countrymen who were neither carefree in body nor in spirit. *The Beggars* (Plate 41) is an intense painting, one that makes us sharply aware of human misery and degradation. The defensively grouped men, the strength implied by their massive shoulders and arms, and their primitive substitutes for the normal means of locomotion are shown with great mastery. The low-keyed color scheme contrasts with the lighter passages of color that unite the group. One more detail you may have noticed: Bruegel, by looking down upon his subject from a standing position, intensified the painfulness of the way the beggars were forced to travel.

PETER PAUL RUBENS

This seventeenth-century painter was a native of Flanders. His life was one of many activities in which he was eminently successful and for which he was widely known. As a schoolboy in Antwerp, he learned to speak six languages fluently, and his interest in art was evident at an early age. In Rubens' day, an artist's training was not complete without a study of the great masters of Italy. While visiting there, Rubens was given commissions to paint for ruling princes and kings. He also traveled as a diplomat and visited the courts of royalty, notably those of Spain and England, in this capacity.

Rubens' fame at the age of thirty was so widespread that the Netherlands requested him to return to his native country. There he established himself in an enormous workshop in Antwerp. The well-known portrait painter, Van Dyck, was among the many famous pupils and assistants who worked with him. His productions included altarpieces and other religious paintings of magnificent content, alive with movement and deep meaning. Huge paintings of mythological subjects include human figures and animals, often in violent action. Still other paintings are based on the lives of his compatriots.

In the painting *Kermesse* (Plate 42), Rubens showed his wide interest in the life of the common people. One feels his pleasure in their natural enjoyment of the traditional harvest festival after a long summer's work. As in all Rubens' works, the color of this painting is clear, brilliant, and luminous, or full of light. His mastery of flesh tones and shadings is unsurpassed. The figures in this painting trace a flowing, ribbonlike movement throughout the scene. They are living for the moment, in a manner characteristic of Rubens' art. Animated and active, they unreservedly savor the joy of life.

The painter's dashing brushwork contributes greatly to the vitality of this painting. However, there is careful drawing and underpainting beneath, in preparation for the final surface treatment of this colorful subject.

REMBRANDT VAN RIJN

Rembrandt, the son of a miller, was born at the beginning of the seventeenth century in Leyden, Holland. His father wished him to attend the university, but he soon left to study painting with the accepted masters of his time. After learning the fundamentals of painting, he embarked on his life work, making a successful career for himself in his early life.

In the small, democratic country of Holland, without the domination of either Church or aristocracy, art was fostered by each citizen's desire to own paintings. In these auspicious surroundings, Rembrandt began as a portrait painter, carefully creating detailed likenesses of his sitters. Soon he began to probe more deeply into the daily life and perplexities of all mankind. In his paintings of Biblical scenes or of people in daily activities, he achieved a depth of emotional expression that gave a unique reality and earthiness to his work. This trend became more profound as he observed life with the wisdom that grew out of his later, personal tribulations.

The Anatomy Lesson of Dr. Tulp (Plate 43) shows a professor surrounded by members of the Guild of Surgeons. In a masterly fashion, Rembrandt combined this assemblage of people into a unified painting. By accenting, subduing, and again emphasizing various areas with dramatic lights and shadows, he directs the eye of the viewer to various sections of the

PLATE 42. Kermesse. *Peter Paul Rubens (Flemish, 1577-1640). Oil on canvas. Pinakothek, Munich (Germany)*

PLATE 43. The Anatomy Lesson of Doctor Tulp. *Rembrandt van Rijn (Dutch, 1606-1669). Oil on canvas. Mauritshuis, The Hague (Holland)*

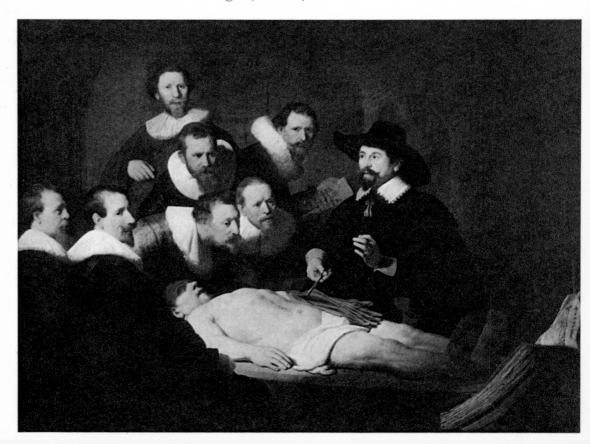

PLATE 44. Interior of a Dutch House. *Pieter de Hooch (Dutch, 1629-1684). Oil on wood. The National Gallery, London (England)*

painting, yet always brings it back to the center of interest. While achieving this unity, he was still able to give each head an individual likeness, and to show in each face an alert and keen interest in the anatomy lesson they are watching.

PIETER DE HOOCH

Large paintings for public buildings continued to be in demand. However, there was an equally strong desire for small paintings, sometimes known as easel paintings, that could be enjoyed in the home. Dutch artists, in particular, painted their friends and neighbors in familiar surroundings, engaged in everyday activities. Pieter de Hooch, a contemporary of Rembrandt, was an important painter of this period, and an artist who could transpose a commonplace scene into a little jewel-like image of life. Notice in his *Interior of a Dutch House* (Plate 44) how interestingly he illuminates his scene with daylight. He used this calm light both to bring out the figures and to suggest the spacious airiness of a simply arranged home. The darks and lights have also been used to bring out the architectural lines of the interior and the figures are interestingly grouped and balanced.

6

Art in a New Light

WITHOUT LIGHT there can be no color, and without color life would be a very drab and dull affair. Because of a growing interest in the possibilities of color for individual interpretation, certain painters experimented with new ways to light their subjects. For example, they used candlelight and studied its effects on models posed in half-lit studios. When painters finally became dissatisfied with indoor painting, they began to paint out of doors. This approach to painting, in which artists became concerned with the effects of outdoor light on color, was an innovation. It aroused a new interest, that of capturing the visible world through the medium of paint.

As a result, the nature of color and light became an important scientific study in the nineteenth century. With the discovery that a light ray could be separated into the colors of the spectrum, just as raindrops form a rainbow when sunlight strikes them, artists began to devise new theories of color. They experimented with ways of placing paint on canvas to produce sensations of radiant light and its effects on the forms it surrounded.

Color was analyzed for all its properties. Vibrant colors, intense and subdued colors, warm and cool colors, light and dark colors, and their many combinations were studied to see how they might best suggest on canvas that which the trained eye of the artist saw in nature. It was found, for example, that contrasting colors, placed next to one another, created effects of nearness in a painting while those which did not contrast gave an effect of distance.

Soon the technique of using broken dabs of color, rather than color

PLATE 45. Arab Saddling His Horse. *Eugène Delacroix (French, 1796-1863).*
Oil on canvas. The Hermitage, Leningrad (U.S.S.R.)

PLATE 46. Crispin and Scapin.
Honoré Daumier
(French, 1808-1879).
Oil on canvas.
The Louvre, Paris (France)

PLATE 47. The Third-Class Carriage. *Honoré Daumier (French, 1808-1879). Oil on canvas.*
The Metropolitan Museum of Art, New York, N.Y. (H. O. Havemeyer Collection)

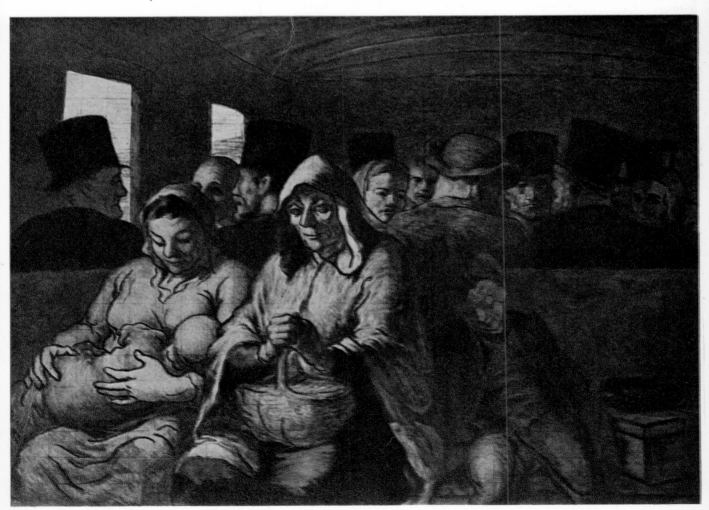

smoothly applied, became popular. Separate strokes of pure color, ribbon-like slashes of color, and blobs and tiny dots of color led to a style of painting that became known as Impressionism.

An artist who preceded the Impressionists once stated, "Gray is the enemy of all painting . . . keep the brush strokes distinct . . . the greater the opposition in color, the greater the brilliance." Although there were many important artists who were forerunners of this movement, Impressionism did not develop quickly, as we shall see.

EUGÈNE DELACROIX

Among nineteenth-century painters before Impressionism, the powerful Delacroix was a great colorist. A Romanticist, or a painter of romantic subjects, he was one of several artists who considered the paintings of his contemporaries to be colorless and highly limited in subject matter. He also felt that their style of painting did not allow them to reveal their personal ideas or feelings.

Delacroix's personal energy and forcefulness are echoed in his work. During a stay in Morocco, the daily life of the Arabs dazzled his color-loving eyes. He sketched innumerable scenes from Arab life and later developed these studies into the striking paintings that made him famous.

Arab Saddling His Horse (Plate 45) first strongly impresses us with the glowing color that flows over every part of the painting. The dramatic sunset, the rich reds and greens so effectively contrasted, and the copper-colored tones of the horse and his rider fill our eyes. In general, Delacroix's color scheme is composed of colors in a low key, or low value. If you place a piece of white paper over a part of the rider's headdress, you will see that while it gives the effect of white, it is actually darker than the white paper.

The figures of horse and rider are posed in a way that suggests powerful and swift movement. Even Delacroix's personal manner of applying paint to canvas suggests action and vitality.

HONORÉ DAUMIER

In the period that preceded Impressionism, Daumier, a nineteenth-century painter, was another important figure. His boyhood was marked by poverty, and at an early age he started to work as an errand boy for the law courts of Paris. There he had ample opportunity to see the hardships met by poor people. Corrupt and unjust practices in many quarters impressed him deeply. The memory of these conditions never left his mind. For more than forty years, Daumier produced drawings, prints, and paintings that attacked those problems. In his zeal for social reform, Daumier has a unique place in the history of art.

People from all walks of life were the subjects of Daumier's drawings and paintings. They might be actors on the stage, as in the painting *Crispin and Scapin* (Plate 46), or they might be ordinary people leading an everyday existence, such as we see in *The Third-Class Carriage* (Plate 47). As a painter of the life around him, Daumier's concern for humanity is clearly revealed. The mood of each painting, the one humorous and active, the other calm and quiet, is established by broad areas of dramatic color. Brilliant contrasts of light and dark give emphasis to faces and figures. One is especially conscious of the power of Daumier's draftsmanship.

ÉDOUARD MANET

In the work of this important nineteenth-century artist, we see the beginnings of Impressionism. Several of Manet's friends and followers later developed some of his theories and techniques into this style of painting.

Manet was interested in the problem of how to suggest natural light. This was of greater importance to him than the actual subject of his painting. For *The Fifer* (Plate 48), he rejected artificial studio lighting and devised his own way of painting the boy's figure. Notice that he used large and almost flat planes of strongly contrasting color. The light, shadowless color of the background helps to establish Manet's type of illumination, which at that time was considered revolutionary. Only the model's face and hands have suggestions of solidity.

EDGAR DEGAS

Degas, another nineteenth-century French painter, is a very popular and appealing figure in the world of art. Although he was influenced by the growing Impressionist movement, and in fact became one of its leaders, he remained very much himself, an artist of unique and independent talent. For one thing, his early training had been in traditional art, and he had

PLATE 48. The Fifer, *Edouard Manet (French, 1832-1883). Oil on canvas. The Louvre, Paris (France)*

PLATE 49. At the Race Course.
Edgar Degas
(French, 1843-1917).
Oil on canvas.
The Louvre, Paris (France)

PLATE 50. Jockeys. *Edgar Degas (French, 1843-1917). Oil on canvas.*
Yale University Art Gallery, New Haven, Conn.

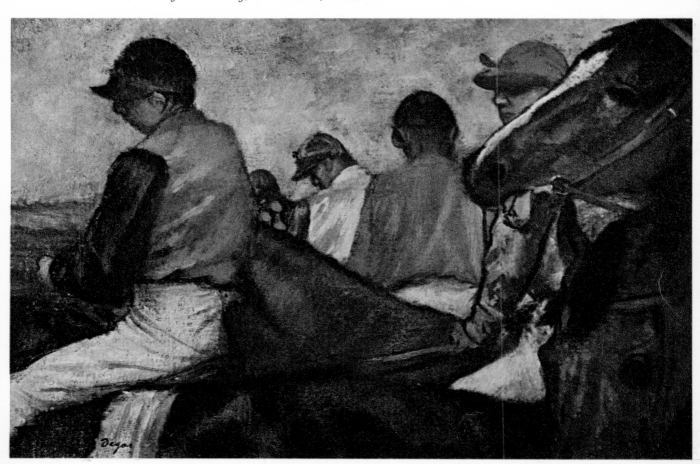

fully learned the importance of draftsmanship. For another, while all his life he made innumerable drawings of people and events that interested him, he did not believe, as the Impressionists did, that the subject had to be constantly before him until he completed his painting. Degas was essentially a studio painter.

Although he often worked in soft pastel, Degas's drawing has power, suggesting figures that were strong and sure, whether they were seen in natural or theatrical lighting. In all his paintings, the figures are bathed in color and light.

Degas's art reflects the life of his times. He found it possible to treat every aspect of that life with the same limitless enthusiasm for color, light, and form. Even a part of a figure or object, whether the back of a jockey or the shape of a hat, or of a ballet dancer's skirt, were seen and selected by him to play an important part in his designed arrangements.

A talent for what might be called frozen motion led Degas to capture striking or significant poses that, as you will see in his paintings, were often diagonal in movement. His use of opposing diagonals added greatly to the vitality and feeling of motion so noticeable in his work.

Another of Degas's innovations was his way of arranging figures in compositions. It startled the public of his time to see a figure deliberately cut off, very much as we are now accustomed to see it cut in candid camera shots where only a portion of a figure may appear, since the rest is outside the camera's range. His use of severed forms made his paintings seem even more like a spontaneous section of life, unforced and natural, as the painter wished it to appear.

At the Race Course (Plate 49) shows how skillfully Degas could reorganize a scene that was spread out in width and depth. Notice, for example, how the horse and rider on the left lead our eyes into the picture, and how the diagonal motion of the smaller horse in the middle distance leads us to the group of riders on the right. They, in turn, bring our attention back to the foreground. Even the diagonal movements of the shadows cast by the horses and their riders were used by Degas to suggest a compact, rather than a scattered scene.

The artist has clearly seen and organized his impressions of the bustle and excitement at the race track. This is a picture of arrested movement rather than one that records the tense swiftness of an actual race. Degas has emphasized the quality of movement he wished to convey by his use of color. Yellows and yellowish browns on the left become redder as they move over to the right-hand side of the painting. There the emphatic red of the rider's blouse strikes a decided note in the color sequence.

In painting *Jockeys* (Plate 50), Degas concentrated on a close-up scene of striking brilliance. No one figure is complete. Perhaps we are first impressed by the dramatic color quality. Then the balanced diagonal movements of color areas attract us. Because details have been deliberately avoided, we can concentrate on the beauty of the design and structure.

The Millinery Shop (Plate 51) is basically angular in design. Contrast is supplied, however, by the plump hat forms that were fashionable in Degas's day. The woman's pose and gesture, together with the luxurious color, establish a mood of feminine charm.

In the *Two Laundresses* (Plate 52), Degas's skill in expressing character is clearly seen. The poses of the women are informal. One yawns wearily; the other, with heavy hand and spirit, is completing her task. Beginning with the diagonal direction of the table, the viewer is led into the picture where vigorous contrasts of curves and angles are to be found. The colors in this painting are those of a well-lighted, airy room.

Degas is famous for his drawings and paintings of ballet scenes. In some of them, the dancers are pictured on the stage; in others we see them in a dance studio. *The Dancing Class* (Plate 53) shows two young girls preparing for their exercises. One is adjusting her costume; the other is practicing a ballet pose. Within the group of four figures, not one is seen in complete silhouette. However, the young girls in their light, long ballet skirts are the most important figures because of their placement and size. The two women help to balance the girls' figures and to give the picture a focal point. Notice how carefully the line movements in this scene have been balanced by the artist. Trace with your finger the diagonal movements from the right-hand side of the picture toward the left-hand side. Then trace those movements that come from the opposite direction.

Although you may think that a painter works only in a chosen painting medium, you may not be surprised to find that many painters have worked as sculptors. Degas was one of these painters. His small bronze statues of young dancers, first modeled in clay and then cast in bronze, are extraordinarily suggestive of the ballet dancer's movements. Even though arrested in motion, they appear poised and ready for the next steps. Degas chose to costume some of his bronze figures with actual materials (Plate 54). This

PLATE 51. The Millinery Shop.
*Edgar Degas (French,
1843-1917). Oil on canvas.
The Art Institute of Chicago,
Chicago, Ill.*

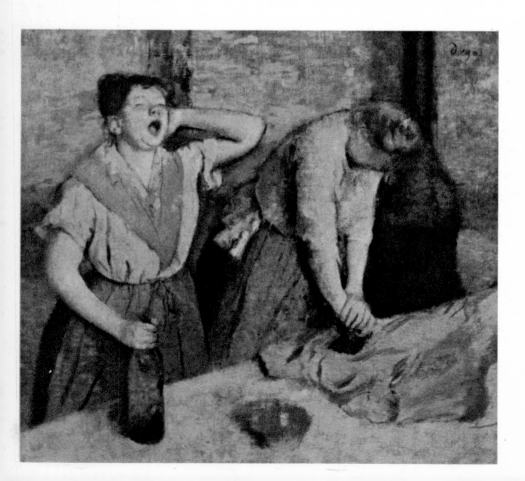

PLATE 52. Two Laundresses.
*Edgar Degas (French,
1843-1917). Oil on canvas.
The Louvre, Paris (France)*

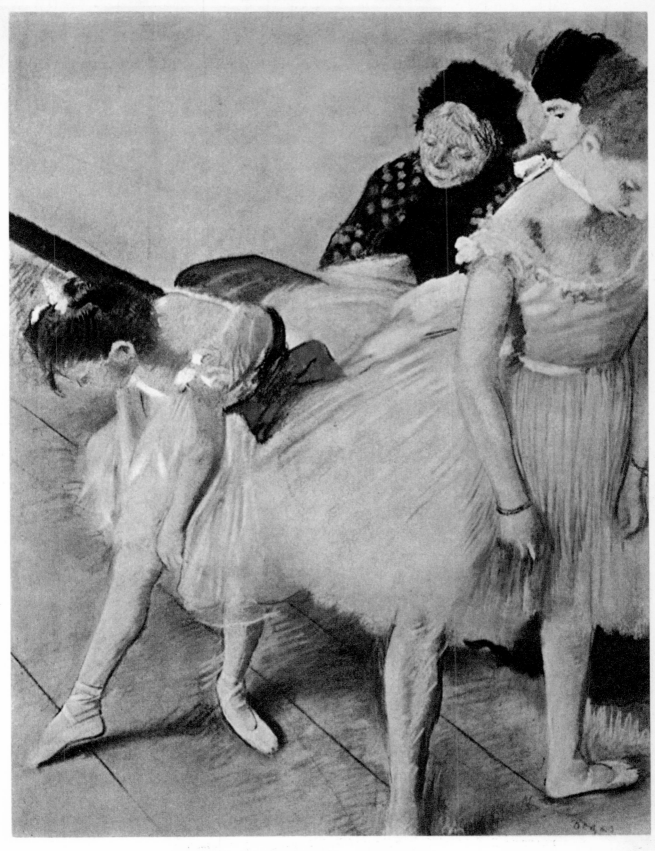

PLATE 53. The Dancing Class. *Edgar Degas (French, 1843-1917).*
Pastel on paper. Denver Art Museum, Denver, Colo.

PLATE 54. Ballet Girl. *Edgar Degas (French, 1843-1917). Bronze.*
The Metropolitan Museum of Art, New York, N.Y.

was his personal way, seldom followed by sculptors, of making his statues appear more lifelike.

PIERRE AUGUSTE RENOIR

This notable nineteenth-century French artist was appreciated in his own time and is widely admired today. The son of a poor tailor, Renoir was apprenticed to a porcelain painter at the early age of thirteen. His task was to paint flowers and figures, but in his spare time he drew from the classical sculptures in the Louvre, the famous museum in Paris. After further work as a copyist, Renoir gladly gave up a commercial career to study art in the studio of a painter. Here he met a few of the Impressionists who were later to become his associates.

In order to catch the hourly variations in the shimmering light surrounding forms outdoors, certain Impressionists made many studies of the same scene at different times of the day. Rather than place color smoothly on canvas, they used broken strokes, or spots, or splashes of color. When you view an Impressionist painting from a distance, as you must, its colors blend into amazing impressions of nature's colors as seen in sunlight, shadow, or halflight. Emphasizing so much the painting of atmosphere and its changing effects on the outside world, the Impressionists did not concern themselves with planned design arrangements, or with solid forms.

Renoir's style, when it reached its fullest development, was broader in scope than that of the Impressionists. He combined the new painting technique of broken color with his feeling for the art of the great masters he had studied at the Louvre. While he, too, produced the momentary impression of flickering light and atmosphere, and their effects upon an outdoor scene, he never lost sight of the total design of his paintings nor of the solid reality of the people in them.

This is evident in the painting, *In the Meadow* (Plate 55). Sparkling light illuminates the skin, hair, and costumes of the girls. The same quality of light shimmers throughout the landscape. Pinks and light blues appear and reappear interchangeably in the meadow and in the trees. This color treatment is very different from the traditional one, where the sky is always blue and the grass forever green. Renoir reveals to us an almost poetic concept of color. He has painted this picture with feeling and imagination, going far beyond the way it appeared in reality.

PLATE 55. In the Meadow. *Pierre Auguste Renoir (French, 1841-1919). Oil on canvas.*
The Metropolitan Museum of Art, New York, N.Y.

OPPOSITE: PLATE 56. The Umbrellas. *Pierre Auguste Renoir (French, 1841-1919).*
Oil on canvas. The National Gallery, London (England)

The study of the human figure gave such pleasure to Renoir that, unlike many of his Impressionist friends, he preferred people to landscapes as subjects for his paintings. In *The Umbrellas* (Plate 56), the feminine charm and natural poses of the figures are typical of the way Renoir saw and reacted to them. The graceful movements of these women, all looking in different directions, and the complex yet natural arrangement of their figures, partially covering or overlapping each other, give us the impression that at any moment they will start to move.

A careful study of this painting reveals how Renoir used his color. Small brush strokes, chiefly of blues, greens, violets, and yellows, move over its surface. Sometimes blended smoothly, at other times contrasted, these brush strokes create figures that are amazingly solid and compact. The surface of the painting glows with color. All of its details are painted with loving care, from the basket on the young woman's arm to the child's costume. Even the figures partially hidden by umbrellas have their own character.

Renoir shows a special interest in conveying to us the feeling and quality of the different materials to be found within the painting. The blue velvet of a woman's jacket shows the richness and softness of that material. Hats, bonnets, and taut umbrellas have all received the painter's careful attention. Even the ground on which the figures stand shows the great importance Renoir placed upon painting every area and surface in such a way as to show its characteristic quality and texture.

It seems that Renoir liked to paint only those people who were happy, healthy, and carefree. This is especially apparent in his *Luncheon of the Boating Party* (Plate 57). The painting radiates the delights of good company and feminine charm. It is pleasant to glance from face to face, from one easy, natural pose to another. Throughout this large canvas, however, there is a carefully designed basic plan. Angular movements form its underlying structure. The porch railing and the shoulders and arms of the figures move in opposite directions. They create distinct and balanced rhythms. The vertical awning poles, glistening bottles, and men's upright figures divide the painting into sections that counterbalance its diagonal movements.

In this as in Renoir's other paintings, including the frontispiece of this book, *Dance at Bougival*, we are conscious of his joy in using color. At times thinly applied and at other times used with dashing effect, the colors reproduce the glowing and shimmering sunlight in which the figures are steeped. Renoir uses colors in a way that fully reveals the solidity of the human figure.

In *Moulin de la Galette* (Plate 58), Renoir again gives full expression to his rich use of color. Dazzling pinks and blues alternate with the darker blues of the men's suits. Nowhere in this canvas is there an area without special color and meaning. Whether it is a man's yellow straw hat seen in the distance, or a girl's lace-edged sleeve, every area leads the eye from one part of the painting to another, as though the viewer, too, were part of this intricate design. The rhythm of curving lines in this painting re-creates the light-hearted mood of the actual scene. Under the subdued lighting of the dance floor, the complexions of the smiling girls in the foreground seem to add a special glow and luminous quality to the entire painting.

PLATE 57.
Luncheon of the Boating Party.
*Pierre Auguste Renoir
(French, 1841-1919). Oil on canvas.
The Phillips Collection,
Washington, D.C.*

PLATE 58. Moulin de la Galette. *Pierre Auguste Renoir (French, 1841-1919). Oil on canvas. The Louvre, Paris (France)*

7

Pioneers of Modern Art

THE STORY OF PAINTING from prehistoric to present days reveals many changes in styles and techniques. One aspect of man's eternal wish to express himself in a highly individual way is his continuous search for different ways in which to work. In classifying or naming changes or innovations of styles and techniques, the terms "movements" or "schools" are frequently used. For example, the interest in Greek classic art that revived during the early part of the nineteenth century resulted in the development of a set, formal style called Neo-Classicism. In the Romantic movement that followed, artists sought to free themselves from the stiffness and restraint of the classic schools of painting. The Romantic artists went to far-off lands for subjects. *Arab Saddling His Horse* by Delacroix, which you have seen in Plate 45, is a fine example of a Romantic painting.

A reaction against romantic subjects brought about a growing interest in the daily life and humble tasks of workmen and peasants. Thus there developed the school of Realists, with such great artists as Courbet and Daumier (whose *Third-Class Carriage* you have seen in Plate 47) as its innovators. They profoundly influenced later artists, each of whom made individual contributions to the development of painting.

Later movements, such as Impressionism, Post-Impressionism, and Expressionism, developed during the latter half of the nineteenth century and the first half of the twentieth. These have directly influenced artists of many countries even up to the present time.

It is important to note, however, that new ideas, new theories, and new experiments in art, as with other intellectual activities, do not appear suddenly at a specified time for all people to see and recognize. Gradual changes take place in the minds of men as the result of many factors. These might be economic, political, or social. When the aristocracy ceased to be the principal patrons of art at the close of the eighteenth century, artists turned to other subjects and other markets. Similarly, the invention of photography and other mechanical and industrial processes have caused profound changes in art. As new ideas crystallize or take definite form, and as artists arrive at their own individual interpretations of ideas or theories, visible signs of change appear. We have seen more rapid changes and experiments in painting during the nineteenth and twentieth centuries than in all the previous centuries since medieval days.

The many new movements in painting that have begun in this century do not mean that there has been a sudden ending or complete stoppage of all preceding styles or techniques. The curtain is not rung down on the final act of an art movement, as it is after the last act of a play. Impressionism, for example, continues in various adaptations in many countries.

However, new movements in painting are generally the result of reactions against old ones. A reaction against Impressionism led to the movement of Post-Impressionism. Interestingly enough, the great painter Renoir, whose work you have seen in Chapter Six, is thought to provide a link between the two movements, because of his concern with design and solidity.

It is clear that new movements in art grow in many directions. They may be thought of as the branches of a sturdy tree trunk that has been formed by the great masters of the past. These men are still a source of strength and guidance, as much for contemporary artists as they were for the students of their own times. Their paintings embody a vast accumulation of knowledge and skill.

An interest in the past has often become the basis for new directions in art. For example, the amazing wood carvings brought to Europe from far countries by traders during the nineteenth century had a stimulating effect on artists. Newly found treasures from remote parts of the world, the Orient, Alaska, South America, and the Pacific islands, have directly influenced modern art movements in European and American art.

Whatever course an artist chooses to pursue, history has demonstrated that his taste is often far in advance of the general taste of his times. The story of new directions in art is one in which public and critics alike have often ridiculed anything that was new and different. Only when people become accustomed to seeing new things done in new ways, when they acquire in some degree the eyes of the artist, do we find careful judgment and greater understanding.

GEORGES SEURAT

Paintings by this French artist, such as *The Circus* (Plate 59) and *Sunday Afternoon on the Island of La Grande Jatte* (Plate 60), are vivid examples of his intense and highly individual studies of scientific color. Seurat applied the theories of broken or separated color to his particular way of painting and headed a movement called New or Neo-Impressionism. He placed tiny spots of color side by side in a precise and exacting way. The colors of the spectrum—red, orange, yellow, green, blue, and violet—if placed properly and seen at the right distance, are blended by our eyes into the colors the artist wished the viewer to see. The term *pointillism* was used to describe this painting technique.

The Circus has an underlying design structure that is characteristic of the thoughtfully planned and highly controlled way in which Seurat worked. The figures of the horse and rider are made prominent by their location and by the line movements that enclose them. Notice how many of the actions or gestures of the other performers draw attention to the yellow-clad rider. In contrast to these line movements, the vertical figures of the audience are firmly placed on horizontal rows of seats. Yellows and oranges, in varying value and intensity, are repeated throughout the painting.

Seurat's interest in design may be seen in the way he chose to present *Sunday Afternoon on the Island of La Grande Jatte*. This scene might well have been painted to suggest the rapid action, confusion, and casual encounters that take place on such occasions. Instead, we see statue-like figures moving in an atmosphere of calm. The use of verticals in figures and trees, of horizontal ground lines, and of restrained diagonals in other parts of the painting is clearly seen. There is also a secondary line movement: the curves repeated again and again in the women's costumes, parasols, and even in a dog's tail.

The figures are seen in both sunshine and shadow. They are arranged in a planned design that suggests a feeling of timelessness rather than change.

PLATE 59. The Circus. *Georges Seurat (French, 1859-1891). Oil on canvas. The Louvre, Paris (France)*

PLATE 60. Sunday Afternoon on the Island of La Grande Jatte. *Georges Seurat (French, 1859-1891). Oil on canvas. The Art Institute of Chicago, Chicago, Ill.*

PLATE 61. The Equestrienne. *Henri de Toulouse-Lautrec (French, 1864-1901). Oil on canvas. The Art Institute of Chicago, Chicago, Ill.*

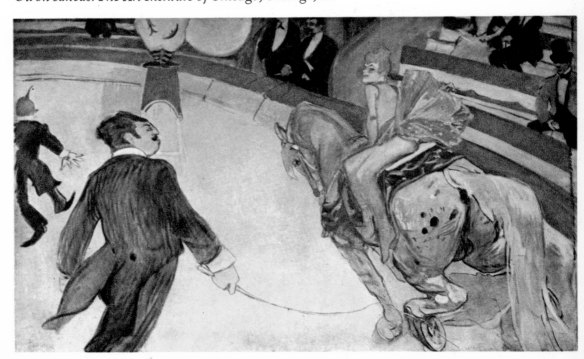

HENRI DE TOULOUSE-LAUTREC

This nineteenth-century French artist enjoyed viewing the night life of Paris, the circuses and dance halls, their audiences and performers. Although using the fresh and sparkling color of the Impressionists, he placed great emphasis on the character of the people he portrayed. *The Equestrienne* (Plate 61) shows his power as a draftsman. With his gift of satire, he characterizes the ringmaster almost to the point of ridicule. However, in presenting the rider, he shows his deeper sympathy for performers who are not glamorous, but hardworking.

Toulouse-Lautrec's compositions of figures, often cut off abruptly by the edge of canvas or paper, his daring, angular lines, and his vivid, at times gaudy, color were innovations that greatly influenced the art of his times.

PAUL CÉZANNE

This great artist, a leader of the Post-Impressionists, has often been called the father of modern painting. Working in France during the nineteenth and early twentieth centuries, Cézanne has inspired countless artists up to and including present times. Although not aware in his lifetime of the important contributions his paintings were to make to the entire world of art, he remained true to his own convictions that the Impressionist manner was inadequate for expressing the structure and solidity of the visible world.

Cézanne withdrew more and more from the company of other artists. He roamed the countryside studying nature and working tirelessly to solve the problems he imposed upon himself. In painting, he was not content to allow nature's forms to dissolve in light and color. He wished to represent them as solid and lasting. The problems of form, three-dimensional quality, and depth were of foremost concern to him.

Story-telling did not interest Cézanne. What he sought was a return to actuality, or as he said, to "reality." In all his paintings, he goes below the surface to develop nature's essential forms and to express their solidity. The *Card Players* in Plate 11 shows how Cézanne concentrated on the planes of objects, relating tones of color to help produce solid structures within a carefully planned design arrangement. Although later theories of abstract and geometric art were in part derived from his work, Cézanne himself never strayed from nature for his inspiration.

The seriousness and deep reflection with which Cézanne approached his work are not only seen in the paintings themselves, but were frequently mentioned by him to his friends. "A painter must bring his impressions to life by means of drawing and color," he said, and clarified this statement by adding that only those theories developed in contact with nature should be applied.

Slowly and painstakingly, and thinking deeply about each brush stroke he set down, Cézanne constructed his paintings on an almost mathematical basis. *Shrove Tuesday* (Plate 62) has for its subject two young men, one costumed as Pierrot, the other as Harlequin. The title of the painting connects these figures with the carnival period just before the beginning of Lent. For Cézanne, these figures undoubtedly had a special character and meaning. One notices the strength of their grouping. It suggests a structure somewhat like a pyramid. The painter's concern with space and the interrelationships of forms and his method of expressing these qualities, make *Shrove Tuesday* one of Cézanne's most important paintings.

VINCENT VAN GOGH

This nineteenth-century Dutch painter is one of today's best-known and most popular artists. His soul-stirring experiences in missionary and relief work in miserable industrial areas of northern Europe led him to the habit of sketching the miners and their families. From there he went to Brussels to study art. His early work, though often crude and awkward, showed his intense feeling for people. Their appearance and surroundings are reflected in his *Potato Eaters,* which you have seen in Plate 12.

A stay in Paris and an association with the Impressionist painters there had the effect of brightening the colors he used, or as it is often expressed, of brightening his palette. Although he was influenced by Impressionism, Van Gogh felt that it lacked solidity and designed organization. His highly emotional nature eventually led him to paint in a way that laid the groundwork for what became commonly known as the Expressionist movement.

Van Gogh moved to southern France, where the powerful sun and lively coloring about him greatly affected his painting. His work became even more intense and colorful. He worked feverishly, and over long periods of time. His urgency can be sensed in the way he applied paint to canvas. He used color in swirling strokes, elongating and crossing them, slashing them on

PLATE 62. Shrove Tuesday. *Paul Cézanne (French, 1839-1906). Oil on canvas.*
The Hermitage, Leningrad (U.S.S.R.)

PLATE 63. Promenade at Arles.
Vincent van Gogh
(Dutch, 1853-1890).
Oil on canvas. The Hermitage,
Leningrad (U.S.S.R.)

PLATE 64. The Night Café. *Vincent van Gogh (Dutch, 1853-1890).*
Oil on canvas. Yale University Art Gallery, New Haven, Conn.

with a brush or palette knife, and even squeezing them directly from tube to canvas. This technique helped him express more vividly the heat and vibrations of the broiling sun as it illuminated the textures of cypress trees, wheat fields, and countless details of roads, people, and vegetation. With his complete concentration on the meaning of every form and color, Van Gogh brought significance to even the most commonplace subjects.

In paintings of outdoor life, such as the freely imagined and composed *Promenade at Arles* (Plate 63), one is particularly aware of the vigor of Van Gogh's painting. The scene is challenging because of its unusual figure arrangements. Characteristic forms of the women of the countryside, of the shapes and colors of its trees and brilliant plants are seen with the artist's well-known intensity of observation. Through vigorous color and lively brush strokes, he emphasizes the particular character of each person and object. At the same time, a tightly organized composition gives full meaning to every part of the painting.

The Night Café (Plate 64) is a powerful interpretation of a subject that is far from lively and attractive. As you have seen in *The Potato Eaters,* Van Gogh was deeply moved and depressed by human poverty. He obviously thought of this café as a place of refuge for depressed and lonely people. Although the gloomy atmosphere is relieved by the concentric circles of light that surround the ceiling lamps, we sense that Van Gogh was nevertheless revolted by the café and its customers. Even the colors—the reds, greens, and yellows—have been deliberately used to convey this feeling.

PAUL GAUGUIN

This nineteenth-century French artist, like his friend Van Gogh, rebelled against what he considered the superficial values of nineteenth-century art. His was a restless spirit. The fascination of art finally led him to a separation from his family and friends, and from his career as a stockbroker. In his search for inspiration and a simpler life, he eventually found refuge on Tahiti in the South Pacific.

Although Gauguin had begun as an Impressionist painter, his style changed with his surroundings. Rich, flat areas of color in decorative patterns revealed the beauty of his tropical surroundings. Figures, animals, flowers, and landscapes are seen as a rich tapestry of color rather than as true-to-life arrangements of color. This is particularly true of *The Ford*

(Plate 65). The brilliance of a full range of riotous color suggests that nature's bounty has been freely given to the tropics. Swirling and tossing watery elements echo the carefree movements of primitive life.

Gauguin also searched for a way to express his feelings for the charm of a primitive existence. For this reason he simplified his drawing and painting to suggest the direct and unspoiled character of an island and its people. His emotional approach toward his subjects is in striking contrast to the scientific approach of Seurat and the theoretical approach of Cézanne. Yet it must not be overlooked that Gauguin drew and painted with knowledge and understanding of the works of past great masters.

Ta Matete (Plate 66) shows how Gauguin used reality only as a starting point from which he proceeded to simplify and redesign at will. In pose and gesture, the seated women remind us of the way the Egyptians presented figures. They are clearly silhouetted and appear in a combined front and profile view. As with all of Gauguin's paintings, a flat, decorative, and rich color pattern enchants our eyes.

Like many of his contemporaries, Gauguin was also influenced by the beauty of line and the decorative designs of Japanese prints which were in vogue at that time. However, his appreciation of the essential values of primitive life and thought, and his sincere desire to reproduce them in a painter's terms, were the ruling force of his life. His retreat from civilization and his style of painting symbolize a return to nature as a primary source of strength and inspiration.

HENRI ROUSSEAU

The majority of painters you have read about in these pages were men well trained in the arts. When young, they studied with recognized teachers. As they grew older, it is evident that further independent study and stimulating contact with the work of past and contemporary artists greatly increased their understanding of new and challenging problems to be solved.

In addition to our admiration for the work of these artists, we have come to find special enjoyment in the work of those self-taught artists known as primitives. Henri Rousseau, who lived and worked in Paris from the middle of the nineteenth century to the early part of the twentieth century, is one of the best known of the primitive artists.

Rather late in life Rousseau gave up his work as a customs official and,

PLATE 65. The Ford.
Paul Gauguin (French, 1848-1903).
Oil on canvas.
The Hermitage, Leningrad (U.S.S.R.)

PLATE 66. Ta Matete. *Paul Gauguin (French, 1848-1903). Oil on canvas.*
Kunstmuseum, Basel (Switzerland)

PLATE 67. The Sleeping Gypsy. *Henri Rousseau (French, 1844-1910). Oil on canvas.*
The Museum of Modern Art, New York, N.Y.

PLATE 68. Burial of Stef Halachek.
Ivan Generalic (Yugoslavian,
born 1914). Oil on canvas. Gallery of
Modern Art, Zagreb (Yugoslavia)

although poverty stricken, devoted himself to painting. The public laughed at his work when it appeared in exhibitions, but other painters, Seurat and Gauguin for example, admired and perhaps even envied his imagination and the childlike freshness of his work. Picasso, already famous, gave a dinner in his honor.

In his *Sleeping Gypsy* (Plate 67), Rousseau painted a full moon to illuminate a background of mountains and a foreground in which a lion is sniffing at the rigid figure of a sleeping gypsy. The bright surface of the mandolin, the carefully drawn folds of the gypsy's garment, the detailed texture of the lion's mane and his glassy eye, and the bright edges of light surrounding each important form all contribute to an atmosphere of dream and fantasy.

IVAN GENERALIC

In Yugoslavia, far away from what we think of as the art world, a group of men with little or no formal training in art have dedicated themselves to "restore" painting by linking it closely to the daily life of their countrymen. Ivan Generalic, first as a boy and now as a recognized primitive or "naive" painter, is a central figure in this group. The *Burial of Stef Halachek* (Plate 68) shows us his instinctive interest in human events and emotions. Whether real or imaginary, the scene is painted with directness and vigor. The figure of the dead man, and the stiff movements of the family, the friends, and the priest reflect their rugged existence in a frozen countryside.

8

New Directions in Art

THE FACILITIES FOR COMMUNICATION between nations, the rapid spread of new intellectual and practical ideas, and the ease with which people can travel to all parts of the world have helped to expand the horizons of contemporary art. Since the world community might now be said to be within speaking distance, a lively exchange and interaction of ideas have notably affected the outlook of artists all over the world. Exhibitions of the work of young artists are now exchanged between countries of East and West and have affected even some of the most traditional forms of art. In painting, for example, it is now difficult to identify any style as characteristic of a country. Thus we speak of its "International Style."

Further study of painting shows that the freedom with which artists have pioneered in art since the days of Impressionism has resulted in many variations of aims and styles. In naming a few of the most familiar movements in painting since Impressionism, one would include Post-Impressionism, Cubism, Expressionism, Surrealism, Abstractionism, Non-Objectivism, and Abstract Expressionism. These, and others less familiar, are all developments of the last fifty years. There have been at least forty "isms" since about 1850, and one must remember that many artists choose to work in styles that existed before Impressionism. Realistic and Romantic painting, for example, can still be found in the work of present-day artists.

One might think that everything to be said in art has already been said so well that it can never be equaled. For example, we might hear, "Who can possibly surpass Giotto, or Rembrandt, or Cézanne in painting?" However, today's artist does not attempt to compete with the past; he feels a

PLATE 69. Three Musicians. *Pablo Picasso (Spanish, born 1881). Oil on canvas.*
The Museum of Modern Art, New York, N.Y.

PLATE 70. Farmer's Wife on a Stepladder. *Pablo Picasso (Spanish, born 1881). Pastel.*
Collection Mme. Cuttoli, Paris (France)

strong desire to probe more deeply into new possibilities for the role of art in relation to his own times.

One important difference between the art of today and that of the past lies in the fact that almost no limitations or rules exist for the modern artist. Rigid regulations, such as those prescribed by the rulers and priests of ancient Egypt, for example, kept the style of Egyptian art unchanged for thousands of years. Whenever art serves a church, a state, or rulers of lasting power, one can recognize a style that artists develop over a period of time and that finally becomes fixed and associated with that period in history.

How vastly different is the situation that faces the artist today! Each artist may choose the ideas he wishes to express and the way in which he may express them. Actually, it is difficult for the artist to make these choices. To understand the problems that artists face, a study of art is essential. Actual practice in some form of art is helpful but not absolutely necessary. Reading, looking, listening, and discussing will help you understand the value and importance, the beauty and expressive quality of many forms of art.

Because we are so close to the art of our times, we may find more difficulty in judging its worth than we do in judging the art of the past. This difficulty by its very nature presents a challenge, one that all young people who have inquiring minds should be happy to meet.

PABLO PICASSO

Although born in Spain, Picasso is generally considered to be a French artist, for he has lived and worked in France for most of his life. At the age of ten he could draw remarkably well. At sixteen his work was exhibited and he was hailed as a child prodigy. This early promise has been fulfilled. His active mind and highly original talents have led him into constant experimentation, not only in the field of painting, but also in sculpture, ceramics, and graphic arts.

In his early years, Picasso progressed through several phases, or periods of painting, such as his "blue" and "rose" periods. *The Gourmet*, which you have seen on page 19, is one of his earlier paintings. In a later period, and after further experimentation, Picasso became a leader in the style of painting called Cubism. Early suggestions of this way of working appeared in the paintings of Cézanne, whose work you have seen in Plates 11 and 62.

Picasso's *Three Musicians* (Plate 69) is painted in the Cubist manner.

The natural figures of the musicians have been broken up into angular shapes, to be altered and moved about at the will of the artist. From the figures of the three men, Picasso elected to paint only the shapes that seemed important to him. He combined these shapes in a flat design that included other interesting elements, such as a sheet of music and a guitar. Unusual inventiveness in arrangements of space, in color contrasts, and in complexity of pattern make this painting outstanding. While one generally thinks of costumed musicians as gay characters, Picasso, through using somber colors, makes them solemn and even stately.

In *Farmer's Wife on a Stepladder* (Plate 70), the composition is made up of flowing lines and shaded or partially transparent planes, a treatment quite different from the flat geometric pattern of the *Three Musicians*. In this pastel painting Picasso worked as an Expressionist painter does, for he was more interested in the emotional than in the descriptive aspects of his subject. You have probably noticed his treatment of the woman's head. It is shown in a double view, that is, it suggests both a profile and a front view. Picasso and many succeeding artists have painted an object as though they saw it from several different angles rather than from one fixed spot, as preceding artists would have painted it. By showing it in multiple views, Picasso felt that he could reveal more about the "truth" of his subject.

In *Night Fishing at Antibes* (Plate 71), Picasso's complex ideas about painting brought him to interpret this subject in a highly individual way. Looking at this important painting, we discover that two men in a boat are spearing fish by lantern light. On the right two girls stand watching them. One has a bicycle and carries an ice-cream cone. Their figures are purposely distorted, that is, altered by the artist from their normal appearance.

While Picasso may have woven many meanings into this painting, there still remains the possibility of enjoying its lively color, its intricate patterns, and its decorative quality. The artist's use of the language of painting in a new and even startling way inevitably engages our attention. The artist is no longer showing us what he has seen or experienced. He is speaking directly to the viewer, using color and design to help us find his meaning.

GEORGES ROUAULT

Rouault, a modern French painter, is considered to be one of the most important Expressionist painters of his time. Expressionists are concerned

PLATE 71. Night Fishing at Antibes. *Pablo Picasso (Spanish, born 1881).*
The Museum of Modern Art, New York, N.Y.

PLATE 72. La Parade (Sideshow Barker). *Georges Rouault (French, 1871-1958).*
Watercolor and pastel. Collection Baugerter, Montreux (Switzerland)

PLATE 73. Large Harlequin with Guitar. *Juan Gris (Spanish, 1887-1927).*
Oil on canvas. Collection Reber, Lausanne (Switzerland)

PLATE 74. The Melon Eaters. *Renato Guttuso (Italian, born 1912).*
Oil on canvas. The Museum of Modern Art, New York, N.Y.

with revealing the "truth," the emotional quality, or the "essence" of a subject, rather than its actual appearance. Once this is understood, the viewer will cease to search for literal representation because he knows that he would be looking for it in vain.

At an early age, Rouault was apprenticed to a maker of stained glass. His interest in art led him to study at night in various art schools. There he met other painters who were later to become famous. Rouault gained immeasurably from contact with these artists. The technique of stained glass, with its black, leaded lines between areas of rich, glowing color, greatly influenced his style. His interest in religious subjects, his strong reaction to social injustices, and his sympathy for human unhappiness formed the basis of his paintings.

Rouault often suggested in his work that people whom we generally think of as lighthearted, may be sad beneath their jolly appearance. In his

112

painting *La Parade* (Plate 72), he started off with the idea of a parade, but it is the spirit and emotion rather than the outward appearance that he wished to capture. As you can see, he did not attempt a pictorial representation of this scene of action and color since he was concerned with its more lasting values.

JUAN GRIS

Juan Gris was also part of the art world in Paris during Picasso's early days there and he, too, became interested in Cubism in all of its various stages. Compare the *Three Musicians* (Plate 69) with Gris's *Large Harlequin with Guitar* (Plate 73). Notice that the former painting is more geometric in style. However, in the latter you can also see evidences of simplification into somewhat geometric forms. The head, neck, and upper part of the figure, the hat, and the guitar are made up of flat shapes, or planes. Areas of subdued color in the background suggest rather indefinite space enclosing the pensive figure.

PLATE 75. Stag at Sharkey's. *George Bellows (American, 1882-1925). Lithograph. Reproduction courtesy of the Brooklyn Museum, Brooklyn, N.Y.*

PLATE 76. Acrobats. *Charles Demuth*
(American, 1883-1935). Watercolor on paper.
The Museum of Modern Art, New York, N.Y.

PLATE 77. Amazing Juggler. *Yasuo Kuniyoshi*
(American, born in Japan; 1890-1953).
Oil on canvas. Des Moines Art Center,
Des Moines, Iowa

RENATO GUTTUSO

The Melon Eaters (Plate 74) by Guttuso, an Italian painter, has some of the simplification of form that you have seen in the previous painting. By breaking up the shapes of the figures and the background without much regard for their natural colors, the painter has created a dynamic pattern that lends great vitality to his subject.

GEORGE BELLOWS

This American artist of the late nineteenth and early twentieth centuries belonged to a group of painters who organized a rebellion against what they believed to be the set tradition of their times. As a member of this so-called Ash Can school, Bellows' chief purpose was the interpretation of the American scene, of its crowds, tenements, slums, streets, waterfronts, and bars. This was a great innovation. The importation of European paintings in the nineteenth century had set a high fashion for foreign styles. No one had seriously thought of the possibilities of a truly American school of art. In this respect Bellows has become an example of the pioneer spirit in art and he is respected for the wholly fresh and genuine way in which he treated American themes. The movement in which he took part formed the basis for a growing interest on the part of artists to develop a native American art based on our country's regional characteristics.

Bellows was particularly attracted to the athletic side of American life. He was not only determined to present its many phases in some form of art, but also to give to that form the qualities usually associated with more serious subjects. *Stag at Sharkey's* (Plate 75) shows a masterly handling of a subject that requires keen observation, analysis, and great simplification. You can see that Bellows selected one dramatic moment in the prize fight and planned a composition based on the movements of the fighters and the referee. Even the spectators' poses are related to the action of the main figures. Angular lines and triangular shapes are repeated throughout the composition. They reach a climax in the powerfully drawn prize fighters. Artistically, figures in violent action are always a special problem for the artist, who must also suggest the natural balance of these figures. Bellows solved this problem very well, as you can see.

Stag at Sharkey's is a lithograph, a kind of print. The artist draws on a prepared stone, and when the stone is properly treated and inked, prints can be made of the original drawing.

CHARLES DEMUTH

This painter was a contemporary of Bellows and also concerned with the American scene. His watercolor painting, *Acrobats* (Plate 76), shows his interest in active figures. Notice how dramatically the acrobat is posed, balancing on the handle bars. Beginning at his toes, the lines of his body unite with those of the other member of the team. Both figures are sharply silhouetted by a spotlight. Compare this painting with *Amazing Juggler* (Plate 77) to see the endless variations that are possible even when artists use similar themes. Naturally they have individual reactions to familiar activities, and they draw or paint them in their own characteristic way.

YASUO KUNIYOSHI

An American painter born in Japan, Kuniyoshi was especially interested in the human figure. He made many studies that stress the design elements of the body rather than its anatomical structure. Often his figures are fantastic, as we can see in his *Amazing Juggler*. Notice the simplicity with which he has suggested the figure. The juggler's deft movements, and those of the objects he is keeping in motion, are skillfully captured. The bicycle, the mask, and the long false nose that is used to balance a ball, each adds humor, inventiveness, and an intriguing quality to the scene.

BEN SHAHN

Shahn, an outstanding contemporary painter, has been continuously sensitive to people who have suffered social injustices or who are handicapped by deplorable living conditions. At times he expresses his feelings about his subjects with harsh vigor; at other times he brings to his drawings and paintings a sensitive and poetic quality. On seeing his *Liberation* (Plate 78), one cannot escape the haunting refrain suggested by its mood. In a stagelike slum scene, littered with rubble, children are briefly enjoying a glorious free-swinging sensation of freedom. This painting plays on one's emotions. Each of us will interpret it in his own way. The spirit of fantasy leaves our imaginations free to discover our own responses to the meaning of the painting.

PAUL KLEE

Because of its directness and simplicity, the art of children and of primitive people has particularly inspired certain artists. Paul Klee, a modern Swiss artist who worked in Germany, is one of these. His way of painting was not the one that he had been taught. It was an approach that he developed entirely on his own. Klee's imagination and his feeling for the fantastic and the poetic led him to find unusual ways of expressing himself. His paintings cannot be considered "pictures" in the usual sense, for they are not concerned with what he has seen or experienced, but rather with what he has felt.

Battle Scene from "The Seafarer" by Paul Klee (Plate 79), showing an odd little man and three fishlike creatures, is drawn very much in the manner of a child. Rich shadings of color and an inventive, sensitive design of lines and shapes attract our eyes to every part of the painting. Though it may seem like solving a puzzle to try to unravel Klee's meanings in this scene of fantasy and stylized design, his new and whimsical way of painting engages our appreciative attention.

ROGER DE LA FRESNAYE

The paintings of this spirited French artist show us how much he liked to reduce his subjects to their basic forms. *The Conquest of the Air* (Plate 80) is centered about two figures that are simply stated and clearly perceived. One man seems to be the planner or designer; the other, the man of action. Notice how the pose and gesture of each one suggests his role. They are given a superman quality by being elevated over earth, rooftops, and other solid structures. By placing them among the clouds, the artist suggests that initial flights through space have already been made. Notice the lively color movement that contributes to the airborne mood of the painting.

SIMILARITIES AND DIFFERENCES IN ART

An interest in art brings forgotten times or unfamiliar cultures closer to us. One's enjoyment of art is heightened when one realizes that artists of

PLATE 78. Liberation. *Ben Shahn (American, born 1898). Tempera on composition board. Collection James Thrall Soby, New Canaan, Conn.*

PLATE 79. Battle Scene from "The Seafarer." *Paul Klee (Swiss, 1879-1940). Watercolor and oil drawing on colored paper. Collection Frau Trix Durst-Haas, Basel (Switzerland)*

the past have seen, experienced, and recorded emotions and activities so like our own. Art forms an interesting basis for comparing periods of man's history. Comparisons enable us to understand other people better, and to appreciate the worth of their accomplishments.

Study *The Chess Players* (Plate 81) and *The Painter's Family* (Plate 82). Do you think that these paintings, which were made about four hundred years apart, have anything in common? The fact that the actual subject, chess playing, interested both artists is only a superficial similarity, although it is interesting to find the same activity, in an almost unchanged form, occupying people in such different times and places. Apart from the subject matter, however, these paintings have obvious differences. It remains to be seen whether or not they meet on any common ground.

First let us examine the setting of Francesco di Giorgio's *The Chess Players*. This fifteenth-century Italian artist painted during the Renaissance period. While Renaissance artists produced superb paintings of religious subjects, their work also reflected their increasing pleasure in painting more worldly activities and enterprises. Artists of this time developed extraordinary skill and versatility in painting lifelike figures. Painting figures to make them appear solidly three-dimensional became a chief preoccupation with artists. They observed and studied the appearance of people and places, filling their memories, and often their sketchbooks, with records of the true nature of life around them. In *The Chess Players* we see the delight that earlier Renaissance painters had in splendid, clear effects of color, and we also see the new feeling of the later painters for the importance of human beings and the world in which they lived.

In looking at this painting, we notice that Francesco di Giorgio was interested in storytelling. Briefly, his tale is based on the fate of the young man who is playing a game of chess. The king has decreed that if the player should lose the game, he must forfeit his life. On the other hand, should he win, he may marry his opponent, who is the king's daughter. What details do you notice in the painting that may give you a clue as to the outcome? You may be sure that it was a happy one for, according to the story, the young lady, having fallen in love with the young man, chose to lose the game.

Let us consider the work of Henri Matisse, a modern French painter whose *The Painter's Family* is on page 122. Matisse was the guiding spirit of that group of artists who were known at the beginning of this century as *Fauves,* or wild beasts, due to the way they used great splashes of pure color.

Matisse, like the other important artists of his time, worked in a highly individual way. While we can say of the Renaissance period that its painters shared common interests and worked in comparable styles, we cannot say this of recent or present-day artists. In terms of art, this is an age of individualism, of trail-blazing, and Matisse was no exception to the spirit of his age. It is interesting to know his method of working toward a finished canvas. He started by making a series of experimental drawings and color trials of chosen subjects. The first of the series was carried out in great detail. Each successive trial painting was progressively simplified. The final result contained only those color shapes that Matisse considered essential to his design. It is important to realize that Matisse deliberately simplified all aspects of his paintings. Without a knowledge of the way in which he worked, one might think his paintings are as spontaneous as those of a child. Actually they are the result of a calculated organization of form and color. It may well be said that Matisse worked from a complex to a simplified treatment of his subject, while Francesco di Giorgio worked from a broad arrangement of shape and color to a more detailed description of his subject

Since it is clear that Matisse's primary interest was in design, we can understand why he did not choose to personalize the members of his family or to suggest any emotional factors that might have led to storytelling.

In spite of the obvious differences in treatment, there are qualities that are common to both paintings. For one thing, Matisse and Francesco di Giorgio alike have expressed a deep interest in life and its human values. A second interesting point of comparison is the fact that a study of the basic design of these two paintings reveals certain similarities. Notice the use of a rectangular shape in the center of each background. In one painting, it becomes a window, in the other, a fireplace. A tall, standing figure at the outer edge of each painting serves to frame the picture as well as to repeat the other verticals. Francesco di Giorgio obtained balance in his composition by repeating large, light yellow areas and by contrasting them with almost equal amounts of black on both sides of the painting. Compare this type of balance with the way in which Matisse solved the problem of attaining balance in his painting.

There is a French proverb, "Les extrêmes se rencontrent," which means "extremes can meet." Clearly there are extremes in the work of these two painters but there are also evidences of common ground. Each man had an interest in the dignity and the value of human activities, and each had an

PLATE 81. The Chess Players.
Francesco di Giorgio (Italian, 1439-1502).
Tempera on wood.
The Metropolitan Museum of Art,
New York, N.Y.

interest in solving in his own way the structural problems that are at the heart of painting.

APPRECIATING ART

Most people are more ready and able to appreciate the beauties of nature than they are to understand and enjoy art, which is man-made. In viewing nature, one needs only eyes to observe. On the other hand, the artist's ideas must be sought out with the mind as well as with the eye. Frequently the artist's manner of painting makes it difficult to understand his ideas. Contrary to the predictable laws of nature, those of art are variable. While they are based to some extent on tradition, they are to a far greater extent determined by the immediate needs and purposes of the individual artist.

As a result, the freedom of the artist to set up his own goals does not always lead to the type of beauty that many people expect to find in a work of art. However, the challenging variety to be found in art should furnish the basis for a personal search into its deeper meanings as a language that for thousands of years has conveyed both universal ideas and personal feelings.

Through a study of art, we can expand our ways of seeing both our immediate world and the world of the past. The observant eye and thoughtful mind of the artist will help bring them into sharper, clearer focus. Art can help us see, study, and enjoy the rich and manifold complexity of the human spirit.

OPPOSITE: PLATE 82. The Painter's Family. *Henri Matisse (French, 1869-1954)*. *Oil on canvas. The Hermitage, Leningrad (U.S.S.R.)*

LIST OF ARTISTS

ANGELICO, Fra (FRAH *ahn*-JEHL-*iko*)
Italian, 1386/87–1455

BELLOWS, George
American, 1882–1925

BRUEGEL, Pieter (BREW-*gell* or
BROY-*gell*), Dutch, 1525/30–1568

CÉZANNE, Paul (*say*-ZAHN)
French, 1839–1906

CHAGALL, Marc (*shah*-GAHL)
Russian, works in France, 1887–

CHARDIN, Jean-Baptiste (*shar*-DAN)
French, 1699–1779

DAUMIER, Honoré (*dome*-YAY)
French, 1808–1879

DEGAS, Edgar (*duh*-GAH)
French, 1834–1917

DELACROIX, Eugène (*duh-la*-KRWAH)
French, 1796–1863

DEMUTH, Charles (*dee*-MYUTH)
American, 1883–1935

DÜRER, Albrecht (DYU-*rer*)
German, 1471–1528

EL GRECO (GRECK-*o*)
Born in Crete, worked in Spain,
1541–1614

GAUGUIN, Paul (*go*-GAN)
French, 1848–1903

GENERALIC, Ivan (*ge-ne*-RAH-*litch*)
Yugoslavian, 1914–

GIORGIO, Francesco di (JOR-*joh*)
Italian, 1439–1502

GIOTTO (JAWT-*toh*)
Italian, 1266?–1337

GRIS, Juan (GREECE)
Spanish, worked in France,
1887–1927

GUTTUSO, Renato (*goo*-TOO-*zo*)
Italian, 1912–

HOOCH, Pieter de (HOKE)
Dutch, 1629–1684

KLEE, Paul (KLAY)
Swiss-German, 1879–1940

KUNIYOSHI, Yasuo (*koonee*-YOH-*shee*)
American, born in Japan, 1890–1953

LA FRESNAYE, Roger de (*fray*-NAY)
French, 1885–1925

LEONARDO da Vinci (*lay-oh*-NAR-*doh
dah* VEEN-*chee*), Italian, 1452–1519

LEVINE, Jack
American, 1915–

MAILLOL, Aristide (*ma*-YOL)
French, 1861–1944

MANET, Édouard (*ma*-NAY)
French, 1832–1883

MASACCIO (*ma*-ZAH-*choh*)
Italian, 1401–1428

MATISSE, Henri (*ma*-TEECE)
French, 1869–1954

MICHELANGELO Buonarotti (*mickel-*
AHN-*jel-oh*), Italian, 1475–1564

PICASSO, Pablo (*pi*-KAH-*so*)
Spanish, works in France, 1881–

REMBRANDT van Rijn (REM-*brant*)
Dutch, 1606–1669

RENOIR, Pierre-Auguste (*renn*-WAHR)
French, 1841–1919

ROUAULT, Georges (*roo*-OH)
French, 1871–1958

ROUSSEAU, Henri (*roo*-SO)
French, 1844–1910

RUBENS, Peter Paul (ROO-*bens*)
Flemish, 1577–1640

SASSETTA (*sah*-SET-*ta*)
Italian, 1392?–1450

SEURAT, Georges (*ser*-AH)
French, 1859–1891

SHAHN, Ben
American, 1898–

TOULOUSE-LAUTREC, Henri de (*too-*
LOOZ-*low*-TREK) French, 1864–1901

VAN GOGH, Vincent (*van* GO)
Dutch, worked in France, 1853-1890

VERMEER, Jan (*vair*-MARE)
Dutch, 1642–1675

GLOSSARY

ABSTRACT EXPRESSIONISM   Effects of lines, shapes, and colors that come from splashing, staining, dribbling, or freely brushing or slashing paint on canvas. Accidental effects are important. The final result is intended to be enjoyed for itself, since, like the best music, it does not represent anything. Like music, it may be quiet, boisterous, gay, somber, and so on. Sometimes Abstract Expressionism is called "Action Painting."

ABSTRACTION (ABSTRACT ART)   Separating or leaving out certain qualities, concentrating on others. In art, departure from natural appearances in order to create new arrangements of lines, colors, shapes, forms, and textures. Such arrangements are not very abstract when they strongly remind us of nature; but they may also be so abstract that there is no resemblance whatsoever. Geometrical abstract art reduces to solids such as cones, cylinders, cubes, and spheres; or to flat arrangements of lines, rectangles, arcs, and discs. Other forms of abstraction lead to irregular, freely invented shapes, colors, and movements, and their effect is more emotional.

ARCHAEOLOGIST   A person who learns about ancient cultures by studying ruins and remains.

ARCHAIC   An early style of art in which human and animal forms are represented in simplified, more or less rigid, shapes. The sculpture produced during the Greek Period from about 700–500 B.C. provides excellent examples of this style.

ARCHITECTURE   The technique and art of building.

ART ERA OR ART PERIOD   An extensive span of time in which the art produced maintains characteristics that are recognizable as a unified style.

ART MOVEMENTS   Particular styles or tendencies that have been directed or formed through theories or shared methods of expression. Examples: Impressionism, Romanticism, Cubism.

ART PROCESSES   Methods of using tools and materials, such as carving, painting, blowing glass, and firing clay.

ART QUALITY   The essential nature of a work of art. Quality depends on the esthetic elements, such as line, form, or texture, and other factors, such as imagination, originality, or superior technique.

CLASSICAL   Stylistic standards that include restraint, simplicity, harmony, and ideal proportions. Refers especially to Greek Art from about 480 to about 400 B.C.

COLOR   This word may be divided into several categories: *Hue* is the actual color as we know it. Primary hues include red, yellow, and blue; secondary hues are orange, green, and violet; and intermediate hues are made through mixing. *Value* refers to the lightness or darkness of hues, and may also refer to black, white, and grays. *Intensity* refers to degrees of brightness or dullness of color. *Color schemes* are the combination or arrangement of varying types of colors: neighboring analogous or related, and opposing or contrasting colors. There are certain descriptive terms that pertain to color: *monochromatic*, or varying tones of one hue; *warm* (reds and yellows), and *cool* (blues and blue-greens); *advancing* and *receding*, the power of color to produce apparent effects of space, volume, and depth; *opaque* and *transparent*, the quality of light penetration.

COMPOSITION   Combination of the elements of a picture into a satisfactory visual whole.

CONVENTIONAL STYLE   Drawings, paintings, architecture, or sculpture made according to accepted or fixed rules, without any attempt to adventure.

CRAFTSMEN   Workers skilled in the use of their materials and tools.

CUBISM   A movement in art in which observed forms were reduced to edges, facets, splintered shapes, and fragmented portions. Whether the objects are near or distant they were handled in the same way. Cubism tends to be geometric in character.

DECORATION   Ornamentation designed to beautify a surface.

DESIGN   A controlled, rhythmic arrangement of lines, shapes, and colors.

DISTORTION   Intentional exaggeration, elongation, or twisting of normal forms to give them greater emotional expression or visual freshness.

DRAFTSMANSHIP   The art of drawing.

EGYPTIAN PERIOD   A time span ranging from the Old Kingdom, about 4500 B.C., through the Middle Kingdom and Empire, to about 1090 B.C.

ENGRAVING   A form of graphic art in which a design or a drawing is gouged or cut into a metal plate. The plate is then inked, and its surface is wiped clean after the ink has been worked into the furrows. Then the plate is run through a press and the image is transferred to paper, producing a print. Many such prints can be produced by repeatedly inking and printing the plate.

EXPRESSIONISM   Emphasis placed by the artist on his inner feeling as he views his actual or imaginative world. The artist tries to paint "haunted," and make it look like a house, for example.

FORM   In *painting*, refers to three-dimensional effects produced either by structural drawing or by surfaces that suggest depth and solidity. Descriptive terms are applied to form, such as basic, geometric, simplified, functional, expressive, complex, and free forms.

FRESCO   Painting that is done on wet plaster with water and pigment.

GRAPHIC ARTS   The arts of drawing and printmaking. Drawings may be in pencil, ink, and crayon, or other graphic media; prints are impressions made from prepared surfaces of wood, metal, or stone.

GREEK PERIOD   The Greek civilization from about 700 B.C. to the first century B.C., extending from the Archaic to the Hellenistic Period.

IMPRESSIONISM   Momentary effects of light and atmosphere, represented in painting by the use of color applied in small dashes which exert their effect when they blend in the observer's eye.

LINE   As used in drawing or painting, refers to the real or imaginary edges or outlines of objects, forms, or spaces. *Contour lines* specifically describe the outer edges of forms. *Line direction* means the total movement of spaces or forms as seen in works of art. Qualities of line vary from delicate to forceful, from precise to vague, from soft to active, from rhythmic to chaotic, from flowing to jerky.

MEDIEVAL PERIOD   Sometimes used to include the Early Christian, Byzantine, Romanesque, and Gothic, ranging from about the fourth to the fourteenth century. Strictly speaking, Medieval includes only Romanesque and Gothic, from about A.D. 1000 to A.D. 1350.

MEDIUM   The material, such as oil paint, watercolor, pastel, chalk, stone, clay, or wood used by the artist to create his work of art. The plural is media or mediums.

MODELING   The shaping of forms in sculpture; and the creation of the illusion of solids in drawing and painting.

MODERN PERIOD   A span of time extending from the later half of the nineteenth century to the present time.

MOSAIC   A technique in which small pieces of colored glass, stone, or other materials are inlaid in a background material to form a pattern; also the decorations made by this process.

MURAL   A term referring to all types of large wall painting.

NON-OBJECTIVISM   Paintings that are devoid of representational content. Generally geometrical. Lines, colors, and textures are freely combined.

PAINTING   The use of a fluid medium for decorating a surface. Although a two-dimensional art when compared to architecture, sculpture, or ceramics, it can express all possible qualities of depth, atmosphere, space, form, and movement, through color.

PATTERN   Design created by a variety of dark and light values, through the interplay and contrasts of colors.

PIGMENT   Finely ground colored substances—ores, clays, stones, or chemicals—mixed with a binder such as oil or water, to make oil paints, watercolors, poster paints, etc.

POST-IMPRESSIONISM   A term used to describe the styles of painting following Impressionism. In contrast to Impressionism, Post-Impressionism sometimes emphasizes form, solidity, and structure (as in Cézanne); sometimes broad color patterning and flowing linear patterns (as in Gauguin); sometimes great emotionalism (as in Van Gogh).

PREHISTORIC   The period of the Stone Age, from about 20,000 B.C. to about 3000 B.C.

PRIMITIVE ART   Art produced by societies in an early stage of civilization, or by any artists who are considered naïve or are unschooled.

REALISM   A style that represents nature as it is normally seen.

RELIEF   Sculpture in which the background surface is in one plane and the foreground figures are raised from it. In *low relief* the background is only slightly below the surface of the foreground. In *high relief* the background is deep and the foreground figures may be almost fully rounded.

RENAISSANCE   Literally, the word means rebirth. The term refers to the discovery and use of classical Greek culture and the beginnings of the modern scientific attitude. It dates from the fourteenth to the early sixteenth century in Italy, and slightly later north of the Alps.

RENAISSANCE, LATE   The development in Northern Europe and Italy following the Renaissance, in the later sixteenth century, leading into the Baroque style of the seventeenth century.

ROMANTICISM   A representational style of art which sought to appeal to human emotions through its discovery of unaccustomed or strange beauty in people, exotic lands, and in the drama of legends and historical themes.

SURREALISM   A modern style of painting which is concerned with the subconscious mind, or the world of dreams. Some Surrealist artists work with a minimum of conscious control.

SYMBOLS   Forms or designs used in art to stand for or to suggest something abstract, such as an idea, a quality, or a condition.

TEXTURE   The quality of materials as they would feel if they were touched. Such qualities as smooth, rough, soft, prickly, slick, and spongy may be included. Painters can suggest such qualities in their paintings.

WOODCUT   A process of graphic art in which the wood is cut away from a wood block, leaving the design in relief. Ink, applied to the raised design, is then printed on paper, cloth, or other materials.

INDEX

133

PHOTOGRAPHIC CREDITS

Foto Alinari, Rome—3, 25, 26, 31; Hirmer Verlag, Munich—
2, 20, 21; Museum of Modern Art, New York, photograph by
Soichi Sunami — 14, 74, 76; Dr. Wolf Strache, Stuttgart — 4;
Photo Vigneau, Editions TEL, Paris—1, 17